DISCOVERING
CHRISTMAS

DISCOVERING CHRISTMAS

A Treasury of
Useful Resources for Churches
and Families

Edited by Jeron Ashford Frame

Judson Press® Valley Forge

Bible quotations in this volume are from: The New Revised Standard Version of the Bible, copyright ©1989 by the Division of Christian Education of the National Council of the Churches of Christ in the United States of America. Used by permission. All rights reserved.
HOLY BIBLE: *New International Version*, copyright ©1973, 1978, 1984. Used by permission of Zondervan Bible Publishers.

"The Story of Christmas" originally appeared as "The Birth of Jesus," "An Event for Everyone," and "Scholars from the East," *The Message*, translated by Eugene H. Peterson. Copyright ©1995, 1994, 1995. Used by permission of NavPress Publishing Group.

"A Prayer Not to Get Lost This Advent," "Advent Beginnings," and "Advent Wilderness" by Jody Seymour are reprinted from *Finding God between the Lines: New Insights from Familiar Passages and Places* by Jody Seymour. ©1997 by Judson Press. Used by permission.

"Christmas Eve with Ivan" from *What a Christmas*. ©Arthur Fogartie. Used by permission of Westminster John Knox Press.

"The Rhinoceros" by Ogden Nash is from *I Wouldn't Have Missed It* by Ogden Nash. Copyright ©1933 by Ogden Nash. Reprinted with permission of Little, Brown and Company.

Library of Congress Cataloging-in-Publication Data

Discovering Christmas : a treasury of useful resources for churches and families / edited by Jeron Ashford Frame.
    p.   cm.
ISBN 0-8170-1293-1 (pbk. : alk. paper)
1. Christmas. 2. Advent. 3. Family—Religious life. 1. Frame, Jeron Ashford.
BV45.D58 1998
263'.91—dc21   98-29126

Printed in the U.S.A.

06 05 04 03 02 01 00 99 98

10 9 8 7 6 5 4 3 2 1

CONTENTS

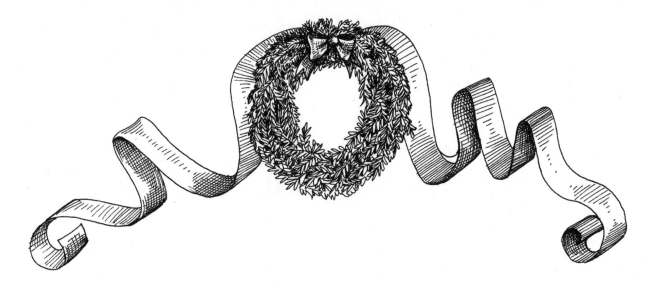

INTRODUCTION

DECEMBER IS FOR MANY THE HAPPIEST AND MOST exciting time of year. For most, it is also the busiest, most hectic time of year. With all the presents to buy, parties to attend, and cookies to bake, the true meaning of Christmas is easily submerged. Many of us get so busy doing the things people do at Christmas that we don't have the time or energy to pause and experience the simple, uncomplicated joy of celebrating the coming of the God-child who brings us peace.

Our hope in developing *Discovering Christmas* is that it will serve as a calm amidst the storm of the season. Its poetry, drama, crafts and recipes, devotionals, stories, and art share the goal of helping churches, families, and individuals experience more fully the true meaning of Christmas.

Despite its essentially spiritual goal, we designed this resource to be as practical and useful as possible.

If you are looking for just the right drama for the children to perform, or just the right program for your family's advent observance, we hope you will find it here. Perhaps you can even create a family or church celebration based entirely on the resources provided herein.

Although it was developed primarily with church and family activities in mind, we trust that individuals who read it on their own will encounter refreshing new ways to understand and experience the meaning of Christmas.

Please consider this book your servant, not your master. Feel free to mix and match its contents. Be creative! Our hope is that you will find it a valuable resource not only this year, but in the years to come as you, along with many others, seek to discover anew the meaning of Christmas.

The Story of Christmas

(Luke 2:1–20; Matthew 2:1–12)
from *The Message*, translated by Eugene H. Peterson

ABOUT THAT TIME CAESAR AUGUSTUS ORDERED A census to be taken throughout the Empire. This was the first census when Quirinius was governor of Syria. Everyone had to travel to his own ancestral hometown to be accounted for. So Joseph went from the Galilean town of Nazareth up to Bethlehem in Judah, David's town, for the census. As a descendant of David, he had to go there. He went with Mary, his fiancee, who was pregnant.

While they were there, the time came for her to give birth. She gave birth to a son, her firstborn. She wrapped him in a blanket and laid him in a manger, because there was no room in the hostel.

There were sheepherders camping in the neighborhood. They had set night watches over their sheep. Suddenly, God's angel stood among them and God's glory blazed around them. They were terrified. The angel said, "Don't be afraid. I'm here to announce a great and joyful event that is meant for everybody, worldwide: A Savior has just been born in David's town, a Savior who is Messiah and Master. This is what you're to look for: a baby wrapped in a blanket and lying in a manger."

At once the angel was joined by a huge angelic choir singing God's praises:

"Glory to God in the heavenly heights,
Peace to all men and women on earth who
please him."

As the angel choir withdrew into heaven, the sheepherders talked it over. "Let's get over to Bethlehem as fast as we can and see for ourselves what God has revealed to us." They left, running, and found Mary and Joseph, and the baby lying in the manger. Seeing was believing. They told everyone they met what the angels had said about this child. All who heard the sheepherders were impressed.

Mary kept all these things to herself, holding them dear, deep within herself. The sheepherders returned and let loose, glorifying and praising God for everything they had heard and seen. It turned out exactly the way they'd been told!

After Jesus was born in Bethlehem village, Judah territory—this was during Herod's kingship—a band of scholars arrived in Jerusalem from the East. They asked around, "Where can we find and pay homage to the newborn King of the Jews? We observed a star in the eastern sky that signaled his birth. We're on pilgrimage to worship him."

When word of their inquiry got to Herod, he was terrified—and not Herod alone, but most of Jerusalem as well. Herod lost no time. He gathered all the high priests and religion scholars in the city together and asked, "Where is the Messiah supposed to be born?"

They told him, "Bethlehem, Judah territory. The prophet Micah wrote it plainly:

It's you, Bethlehem, in Judah's land,
  no longer bringing up the rear.
From you will come the leader who will
    shepherd-rule my people, my Israel."

Herod then arranged a secret meeting with the scholars from the East. Pretending to be as devout as they were, he got them to tell him exactly when the birth-announcement star appeared. Then he told them the prophecy about Bethlehem, and said, "Go find this child. Leave no stone unturned. As soon as you find him, send word and I'll join you at once in your worship."

Instructed by the king, they set off. Then the star appeared again, the same star they had seen in the eastern skies. It led them on until it hovered over the place of the child. They could hardly contain themselves: They were in the right place! They had arrived at the right time!

They entered the house and saw the child in the arms of Mary, his mother. Overcome, they kneeled and worshiped him. Then they opened their luggage and presented gifts: gold, frankincense, myrrh.

In a dream, they were warned not to report back to Herod. So they worked out another route, left the territory without being seen, and returned to their own country.

ADVENT
DEVOTIONALS
For Families and Churches

The Advent workshop readings on the following pages are
easily adaptable for both families and churches. Use the
Sunday liturgies as you light the Advent candles each week.
Read the daily devotionals on your own or during family times
or meal times. Welcome Christmas with a reading of the
beautiful meditation "Come and Worship" on Christmas Eve.
Then join together on Christmas Day with family, friends, or
congregation to celebrate the coming of Christ into the world.

A Family Liturgy for the First Sunday in Advent

by Rev. Luther C. Pierce

READER 1: Today we think about HOPE. We remember Paul's famous line: "Now faith, hope, love abide, these three." Hope is central to both faith and love. It is one of God's greatest gifts.

READER 2: *Read Romans 5:1-5.*

READER 3: Today well lived makes tomorrow a vision of hope.

CHILD: I light this first candle of Advent and name it HOPE.

READER 4: Thank you, Lord God, for Jesus, the source of our hope. As we prepare to celebrate his birth, we will remember that he came to show us what you are like. Today, let Jesus raise us above every problem and sadness, for we have seen your glory in him and we have hope. Amen.

ALL SING: "O Little Town of Bethlehem"

Time for a Change

See, I am making all things new.
Revelation 21:5

LIKE A STICK IN A BICYCLE SPOKE, CHRISTMAS INTERRUPTS OUR PELL-MELL RACE THROUGH LIFE. It catches us in the midst of the half-read page, microwave meals, answering machine messages—even videos of a flickering fire in a fireplace for those who have no time for chopping, gathering, and stacking. When life becomes bonkers or boring, it's time for a change.

Advent offers us real time. At the end of each Classic Comics is the suggestion, "Now that you've enjoyed this condensed version, why not try the original?" It's hard, these cluttered days, to remember what that kind of original life might be. Words like *abundant, stillness,* and *loving* come nostalgically to mind.

Choose a spot where, these next weeks, you can prepare to regain this abundant life. Share thoughts with God, ask questions, listen, savor the silence, trust the stillness. The promise we celebrate at Advent is that God can make all things new, even our compressed lives.

Margaret Anne Huffman

Lost in the Noise

Be still, and know that I am God!
Psalm 46:10

I HAVE LARYNGITIS, THE DOCTOR SAID, AND MUSTN'T TALK. Just rest and be still and quiet, she prescribed. It's an alien proposition, especially this time of year. Anxiety joins fever to worsen my malaise.

And, voiceless or not, if I wanted to be still and quiet, where would I go? We're drowning in noise—at the supermarket, in the car, even at the gas pump. Silence is suspect, an empty hole to be filled. Yet we're invited, urged, to "be still and know"; the two go together. After all, SILENT is the anagram of LISTEN.

Be careful who and what you invite into your quiet places, for sweet solitude can be easily bruised.

Margaret Anne Huffman

A Prayer Not to Get Lost This Advent

O GOD, WE GET LOST almost every year at this time.

    Lost trying to remember . . .
    Lost trying to buy our way out . . .
    Lost trying to finish the list . . .
    Lost trying to make it the best Christmas ever.

Save us, God, as only you can do. Save us from the wilderness of malls, the wasteland of plastic, and the desert of re-creations of Christmas past.

Pull us aside and remind us that we must tiptoe to the manger if we are to hear the sounds of Christmas. He will come again, won't he?

Wrestle us away from the depression of not having enough

      time
      love
      money.

Save us with the soft cry of the Child who knows we still need silent nights. You know how to find us when we are lost. Make us remember that what matters is love given.

We pray in the name of the Child who came for the lost child in all of us. Amen.

Jody Seymour

Getting Down to It

Put away your former way of life . . . clothe yourselves with the new self.
Ephesians 4:22–24

AN ORANGE ANCHORED THE CHRISTMAS STOCKINGS OF MY EAST TENNESSEE CHILDHOOD. Piled on top of it were an apple, new pencils, and a silver dollar. I saved the orange for last, not because of its value but because of the difficulty in eating it.

We spend a lot of "faux" time this month, bluffing our way through what must be done, never quite getting around to what we really want. Like peeling an orange to get to its essence, finding the heart of Christmas is also hard work. Both involve getting rid of the excess.

What would we find if we "peeled" our holidays?

Let's begin by paring our "to-do" lists, believing that reduced pressure in no way diminishes the value of gifts we give or parties we throw. For in doing less to find more, we release the zest of Christmas, like the pungency of an orange, that lingers long after the fruit is eaten.

Margaret Anne Huffman

Secrets

I am bringing you good news of great joy.
Luke 2:10

I SENSED TROUBLE BREWING. Two of my daughters were in one corner of the room, whispering to each other and smiling. The third daughter was in another corner, convinced that she was the one being whispered about. In our home (and I suspect in most homes with three daughters) whispering secrets in the presence of the "whisper-ee" is grounds for legal action.

I waited for the yelling to begin. It didn't. Something was clearly wrong with this picture. Then the solution to the mystery came to me. It was the Christmas season. This time of year, whispers take on a new identity. They are not whispers designed to make fun of or embarrass someone. They are good whispers, about what to get someone else for Christmas.

Let us revel in the joy of this season that enables us to see the same events and circumstances with kinder eyes, that transforms our hearts, our minds, and even our whispers.

Randy Frame

Of Two Minds

For everything there is a season, and a time for every matter under heaven.
Ecclesiastes 3:1

THE WRITER OF ECCLESIASTES WAS WRONG ABOUT A TIME FOR EVERYTHING—HE NEVER SAW MY LIST! I'm about one project shy of a real overload.

Like Mary and Martha, I'm "both/and" about the busyness issue. It is the hot topic these days, with books, calendars, and experts for people who do too much, try too hard, push too long.

It was this relentless busyness that caused Jesus to chide his friend, Martha: "You are upset over all these details!" Jesus knew that the most important kind of busyness involved relationship. Saying "yes" to relationship and "no" to empty busyness allows us to be in the sacred places when children learn to walk, read, drive; when mates invite or friends call; when nature displays its miracles.

We remember that God took chaos and made it into cosmos. How? Through relationship. It's still happening. Come, sit and join the conversation.

Margaret Anne Huffman

A Family Liturgy for the Second Sunday in Advent

by Rev. Luther C. Pierce

READER 1: Today we think about LOVE. We remember that John tells us, "God is love." We know that Christmas tells us how much God loves us. The thought makes us very happy and makes Christmas very special.

READER 2: *Read 1 Corinthians 13:4–7.*

READER 3: To love as Christ loves is to let our love be a practical and not a sentimental emotion.

CHILD: I light this first candle of Advent. Its name is HOPE.

CHILD: I light this second candle of Advent and name it LOVE.

READER 4: We love you, Lord God. Bless our love that it might be a practical expression of our faith. Help each of us to love someone or something that we dislike. Yes, we want to "love our enemies" as Jesus commanded. Help us make real this brave prayer. We ask through Christ our Lord. Amen.

ALL SING: "Silent Night"

Ready, Set . . . Stay?

I know the plans I have for you . . . plans for your welfare and not for harm.
Jeremiah 29:11

IT'S AN EXTRAORDINARY WINTER HERE ON MY WOODED HOOSIER RIVERBANK. Daffodils have appeared three months early, neither geese nor hollyhocks have completely left, and it's still not cold enough to need our down comforter.

What's going on here?

The world is getting ready to end, say some. Climate changes are just the tip of the iceberg, so to speak, pushed ahead of the new millennium like a snowball from hell. Can it be true? Is life as we know it soon to end?

No one knows, despite the hype, for God doesn't perform on cue for those who claim to hold truth, like a conjurer's card, up a sleeve. As for us, what shall we do? Exactly what we're doing right now: preparing with hearts full of hope. The Christmas Baby, like all babies, is a sign of God's continual re-creation; all the promise we need right now.

Margaret Anne Huffman

Advent Beginnings

The water that I will give will become in them a spring of water gushing up to eternal life.
John 4:14

BEFORE THE EVERGREEN OF HOPE THERE APPEARS THE WILDERNESS OF WAITING. We desire to pour some water down our throats quickly, but first our thirst must be noticed.

"No one knows the hour of his coming," go the ancient words with dusty sounds. And so we hurry around the "end" and create our own jingle-bell beginnings.

But the birth requires a waiting, unless it is a molded plastic baby that we really desire. The unwrapped manger child is not the real thing. Remember.

Only through the Advent wilderness, where thirsty pilgrims journey, can the child who comes "out back" be found and rediscovered to be ours. Remember.

The Creator of all time still holds the ends and wonders if we will take the time to prepare a highway for a king who has come to take something away before he gives. Remember.

The waiting wilderness leaves us dry so that later we may truly taste the water. Those who want to be pilgrims and not simply passersby need to not hurry by the Advent wilderness. In such haste the Christmas Child will be missed. Remember.

Jody Seymour

Excuses

Do you want to be made well?
John 5:6

CONFRONTED WITH THE LIVING CHRIST, THE FELLOW AT THE BETHESDA POOL PONDERS THE QUESTION THAT CHRISTMAS asks of us now: "Do you want to be different?"

Uncertain, we wait before answering. But that's okay; after all, isn't Advent about waiting? Time to ask ourselves: waiting for what?

Are we waiting for new life and movement? Waiting for refreshed hope? A companion? Waiting by changing direction, focus, and goal?

Or are we, like the pool-sitter, waiting for something or someone else to do it for us rather than picking up the pallets of our overdone lives and dulled dreams and scooting toward the swirling waters of grace that flow to us this season? It's easier to sit and wait than get up and go.

Do we want to be different? Time to answer . . . for Christ is waiting.

Margaret Anne Huffman

Advent Waiting

My soul waits, and in his word I hope.
Psalm 130:5

WAITING—fingers slowly tracing
    love across the stretched flesh
      on an abdomen full of hope.

Waiting—some nameless innkeeper
    ponders how angry travelers
      will find enough room.

Waiting—shepherds' thoughts escape
    toward empty heavens soon to
      be full of angel voices.

Waiting—all creation like some
    spinning cocoon filled with
      wings of anticipation.

Waiting—on her child of "no room"
    whom shepherds will declare as
      the fulfillment of all creation.

Waiting—so must we
    on birth, and crowds, and common
      folk who announce God's surprise.

Jody Seymour

Unexpected

As you did it to one of the least of these . . . you did it to me.
Matthew 25:40

MY NURSE FRIEND APOLOGIZED WHEN SHE ARRIVED LATE FOR LUNCH. A woman had come to the clinic without an appointment. Frightened and "without resources," code words for poor and no insurance, she had a lump on her breast. A bad one, my friend could tell. There were, however, no referrals to be had. No one would take even a diagnostic look once the patient's "situation" was explained. Tight schedules, don't you know.

Buttoning her blouse, the woman said simply, "Then I'll just have to die."

That was a month ago. My friend found money for a mammogram but lost the woman, who is no longer at the address she gave. Somewhere in a holiday crowd is a woman enjoying her last Christmas.

This is the season of the unexpected, those strangers and visitors who usually arrive at a bad time, not dressed as we expect nor asking what we assume the Incarnate would ask. They are the reason for the season; we are the only ones who can make it work.

Margaret Anne Huffman

I Gave Last Week

Every generous act of giving, with every perfect gift, is from above.
James 1:17

A MIDDLE-AGED MAN GOT OUT OF HIS CAR AT THE GROCERY STORE UNEASILY. The first sound he heard was the sound of a Salvation Army bell. As he approached the door, he avoided eye contact, but could not escape the sound. At the last second, he turned and said, "I gave last week." The bell ringer responded, "Thank you."

But on his way out, the man got uncomfortable again. Finally, overcome by self-imposed guilt, he put a dollar into the pot, then quickly made his escape.

Soon after, a second man emerged from his car with a big smile. He walked boldly toward the bell ringer as he reached into his pocket. "Twenty years ago," he said in accented English, "my family and I were refugees. Everything we needed we got from the Salvation Army. And every chance I get, I give back."

Two givers. Two gifts. Two totally different reasons for giving. Let us always remember that the Christ Child came to free us from guilt, enabling us to give with joy.

Randy Frame

A Family Liturgy for the Third Sunday of Advent

by Rev. Luther C. Pierce

READER 1: Today we think about PEACE. Jesus said, "Blessed are the peacemakers." We speak of God's beautiful vision for his creation by using the Hebrew word *shalom*. It will be the time of peace and plenty for all of creation when war is past. Yes, God wants us to be peacemakers.

READER 2: *Read Isaiah 9:2–7.*

READER 3: Peace, like every other rare and precious thing, doesn't simply come to you. You have to search for it and earn it.

CHILD: I light this first candle of Advent. Its name is HOPE.

CHILD: I light this second candle of Advent. Its name is LOVE.

CHILD: I light this third candle of Advent and name it PEACE.

READER 4: God of shalom, we know that you want us to be peacemakers. Forgive us for the many times we create conflict and not peace. Bless our nation with your vision of peace. Strengthen us with your wisdom and Spirit as we seek peace in your world. We will always hope for peace, using love as our best way to achieve it. Hear us as we pray in the name of the Prince of Peace. Amen.

ALL SING: "Hark! The Herald Angels Sing"

From Fear to Trust

God has sent the Spirit of his Son into our hearts, crying, "Abba! Father!"
Galatians 4:6

HE WAS SUCH A TINY BLACK CAT THAT HE MADE NO FOOTPRINTS WALKING IN THE SNOW TO EAT FROZEN BREAD AT OUR bird feeder. Too cold to fight, he let me catch him. We named him Blackberry Winter, and in a year's time we have tamed and reclaimed him from whatever horrors dumped him in our woods. I smile now through a yawn, for at 2:00 A.M. today, he sat in the sleet, meowing beneath my window, certain I would crawl from my bed, forgive him for staying out, let him in, and overlook him drying cold, wet fur by twining around my ankles.

It's in that same spirit of trust we approach God, thanks to Advent. Our cries have been heard, we've been spotted. I'm sure Blackberry, had he been in the Bethlehem stable, would have joined the legendary animals calling out "Noel!" We echo it, for their startling song of Love-Come-Among-Us is also ours: we've been found, taken in, changed. Each day offers dozens of opportunities to respond in kind, to be God's hands and feet, bringing one another in out of the cold, continuing work begun in a stable.

Margaret Anne Huffman

Advent Wilderness

Make straight the way of the Lord.
John 1:23

ROADS BENDING AROUND the dryness of our souls
A dripping wet messenger steps onto the path.
"Prepare!"
What baptism is this you offer for our parched places?
Your water seems hot as if warmed by some judging fire.

Who is this one of whom you speak who shall wash and reap?
Is this not more arid wilderness—more rules like salt in our mouths?

Bathe us in spite of our fears—
Other waters have left us waiting.
Fill our wilderness with your promise
of one who is to come
and we shall wait
and wonder.

Jody Seymour

Thoughts That Go Bump in the Night

Be renewed in the spirit of your minds.
Ephesians 4:23

THE NEWEST YOUTH GROUP MEMBER WAS NERVOUS AS HE TRIED TO MEMORIZE THE OBSTACLE COURSE OF CHAIRS. He was the first in line to play "Maze." He had to navigate—blindfolded—the chairs and reach the other side where the rest of the group waited. "Ready, set, go!" they shouted. Cautiously off he went.

Quickly and silently, the group removed the chairs, leaving the new guy to navigate a maze no longer there!

How like Christmas . . . how like life. We avoid obstacles that exist only in our minds. We're afraid to change our routine, learn a new skill, call an estranged friend, try new routes, take a stand—whatever it is that we'd really like to do but don't because of obstacles. *Perceived* obstacles. Perhaps we shouldn't avoid chairs until we run into one! And if we do, maybe it's just a place to stop, consider, weigh options, and change directions.

Christmas takes off the blindfold, showing us a clear path through valleys to our heart's destination. It is God, a burr under the saddle, urging us forward.

Margaret Anne Huffman

Slow Learners

He is our peace.
Ephesians 2:14

THERE'S TALK OF WAR AGAIN. I confess I only pay full attention anymore when war involves me, mine, us, ours. The news is full of wars everywhere, over anything with anyone. We fight small wars, too, on roads, in families and marriage beds, at work and play, in church, courthouse, and Capitol. These are mean-spirited times.

No wonder the people who walked in darkness that long-ago Bethlehem time wanted a mighty warrior messiah. We could use one now, from the sound of things. But is that what we've learned in all these years? That war works? That peace is impossible? If so, why do we celebrate the birth of the Prince of Peace year after year? Are we dim-witted . . . or hopeful?

The answer is as close as a spiderweb in the corner. It reminds us that no hope is too small. It is *kiven*, Hebrew for "hope: to twist or twine like a spider web". Let this be the quality of our hope: amazing strength that looks at first like a fragile, insignificant strand. Yet think what it does for the spider. Think, too, what could happen if we twisted our tiny-stranded hope into sturdy ropes of commitment to finding common ground.

Margaret Anne Huffman

Advent Turnings

The earth shall remember and turn to the Lord.
Psalm 22:27

GOD, weary of the noise of
    pleas unheard
Decided to deafen the world
    with a night of silence.

Mary, weary of a journey
    too long
Whispered, "Let it be so"
    and birthed the stable child.

Shepherds, weary of tending
    sheep who would be lost
Knelt before a manger because
    angel dust filled their eyes.

Now you, weary of traffic and
    lists and expectations
Must work to listen and hear again
    a night of silence.

Jody Seymour

Bit Players

Blessed are the eyes that see what you see!
Luke 10:23

PAGEANT PRACTICE IS GOING WELL. Songs soar, costumes fit, props blend. The cast is small and there are few lines to learn, for now, as then, it's mostly bit players in the Christmas drama.

We sit in the wings and wonder why so few saw Jesus.

There should've been standing room only in that dark stable. Did the star appear only to those few we read about? Or are they the only ones who dropped what they were doing and followed it until it stopped? And of those who heard the angel's invitation, why did so few RSVP with action?

This year appears likely to be little more than a re-run, for we, too, are easily sidetracked and never quite make it to the manger. Focused on a distant star, we miss seeing it stop over the nativity going on all around us. Yet Christ daily comes to us wherever we are; the cast call never changes. What part shall we play: the ones who went . . . or the ones who didn't?

Margaret Anne Huffman

A Family Liturgy for the Fourth Sunday in Advent

by Rev. Luther C. Pierce

READER 1: Today we think about JOY. Christmas is a joyful time, especially when we remember that it is more a time of giving than of getting. The book of Hebrews speaks of Jesus "who for the joy that was set before him endured the cross." This is the kind of joy that will bless our Christmas.

READER 2: *Read John 15:1–11.*

READER 3: There is a tremendous joy in giving. It is a very important part of the joy of living.

CHILD: I light this first candle of Advent. Its name is HOPE.

CHILD: I light this second candle of Advent. Its name is LOVE.

CHILD: I light this third candle of Advent. Its name is PEACE.

CHILD: I light this fourth candle of Advent and name it JOY.

READER 4: Joyful God, we are so happy as Christmas approaches! We look forward to worship on Christmas Eve; to the beautiful music of choirs, to the stirring proclamation of the Good News of the Savior's birth. We anticipate the joys of giving and receiving gifts, symbolic of your gift to us. Our feasting will proclaim our joy in our Lord. Fill us with your joy, O God! Amen.

ALL SING: "Joy to the World!"

From Darkness to Bloom

I will give you the treasures of darkness.
Isaiah 45:3

HYACINTH BULBS SIT IN A BOX UNDER MY DESK ON THIS SHORTEST DAY OF THE YEAR. I keep peeking, but they're still just root and promise. It seems unnatural to leave them in the dark. However, they'd be all pale leaves and no blossom if not given the darkness they need.

How we fear darkness, the places of secrecy, dormancy, and decay. We forget that some darkness is a crucial half of creation, a necessary break, when body, mind, and spirit are nourished. Even when darkness is despair where monsters, real or imagined, lurk, dawn is guaranteed. Day follows night as surely as bloom follows bulb, the promise of this season. For in a few days, we, like dormant bulbs in a dark box, get another chance to grow when Hope comes to us, offering opportunities undreamed.

Margaret Anne Huffman

Forgive and Forget

Guide our feet into the way of peace.
Luke 1:79

I HEARD A CHRISTMAS SERMON ONCE THAT DEFENDED—OF ALL PEOPLE—THE INNKEEPER. I'd always thought of him as something of a villain, or at least as someone who was selfish and inconsiderate. But according to the sermon, the poor guy was an innocent victim of circumstance. After all, he had no choice but to give priority to those who'd made reservations and who were probably already tucked away in bed. Plus, he had no way of knowing who he was turning away.

If I had been Mary or Joseph, I suspect that one day I would have gone back to that innkeeper to remind him of the big mistake he'd made and maybe rub it in a little. But I don't think they were the type to hold grudges. Certainly Jesus was not the type.

This is the season of joy. It is also, sadly, a season of grudges, resulting from unhealed wounds and unsettled grievances. Maybe remembering the innkeeper will help us to remember the example of Christ, who taught us to forgive and move on.

Randy Frame

A Second Look

Unless you become like children . . .
Matthew 18:3

"WHY," SHE ASKED, "ARE ALL THE FIGURES IN YOUR NATIVITY SET LYING DOWN?"

I looked where she pointed. It was a topsy-turvy scene in my cardboard stable where shepherds, camels, and Magi were all upended feet and elbows and angels wore halos at a rakish tilt from lying on the ground.

"Because," I confessed, "the grandbaby loves to play with them and she's tucked them in for the night."

"Well," my visitor sniffed, "it's not proper."

What, when you think about it, is proper about Christmas? There's a baby born illegitimately in a dark, dank stable attended by farm animals, a few ragtag shepherds and bemused astrologers. All this to bring us, the most improper of all, a gift of renewal.

Improper but real. That's the true decor for Christmas. For just as it only takes a toddler snuggling a plastic sheep to make it real, releasing its woolly warmth, it takes a Babe to bring us to life.

Margaret Anne Huffman

Still, Still, Still

The Lord waits to be gracious to you.
Isaiah 30:18

STILL THE MANGER SCENE
    can adorn our tables
        instead of our lives.

Still the world wonders
    if perhaps a baby born
        amidst the straw is the one.

Still we have the chance
    to allow the child
        to be "Christ the Lord."

Still, still, still . . . God
    waits each year
        to see what will happen
            when the manger
               is unwrapped.

"O Holy Child of Bethlehem
    be born in us today."

Jody Seymour

Star Bright, Is That You?

O Lord, how majestic is your name . . .
Psalm 8:1

NOT ALL THAT BLINKS IN THE CHRISTMAS SKY IS A STAR. Nearly 9,000 things share space with stars, according to the U. S. Space Command. Things like nuts, bolts, and chunks of satellite. Always searching for signs and stars to follow, especially this time of year, we need to avoid space junk lest we get led astray.

How can we tell the difference? Only one Star changes lives.

We get a fresh vision of it at Christmas. All we need do is look through eyes of faith beyond our busy schedules and distractions, pains and worries, to the message in the sky: God is. We gain reverence and a sense of purpose when we recognize that what we do does not make us God! We fling junk into space; God sets planets, moons, and stars into orbit. At best, we gratefully take what God has given us and rearrange it so it can continue the work of creation.

Go outside tonight and open the eyes of your soul to search for the Christmas star. It is there.

Margaret Anne Huffman

Come and Worship

A Christmas Eve Meditation

by Jeffrey D. Jones

THERE IS A CERTAIN STILLNESS to this moment
    the journey is over, a place of rest has been found
    the pain of birth is yet to begin
    there is a certain stillness to this moment

We know it will not continue so
    we know the journey will begin again—all too soon
        forced by fearful rulers whose only desire is to protect their position and their power
    we know the struggle to live and grow and learn and love will once again commence
    we know, too, that for the child born this night it will lead to conflict and controversy
        to suffering and to death
    we know that life will take its toll on him
        as it does on everyone
            as it has on us
    we know all that, but now there is stillness
        now we can rest and know a peace more profound than any other
            the peace that comes from knowing God is in this moment

In the quiet, in this God-given moment, the child stirs—the time has come
    there is pain, contracting pain—as all of life contracts
    into this one moment through
        which it must pass
    there is pain—all creation groaning in the pangs of childbirth
    there is pain
    and God is here now, too—in the pain as well as in the peace
    God is here now, too

Because God is here the pain has a new dimension to it
    there is hope in the pain
    there is love in the pain
    there is joy, even joy, in the pain

Yet the pain increases, its intensity grows—it becomes greater, and greater still
     until it is fulfilled
     fulfilled in the birth of newness and wonder
     fulfilled in the birth of a child who is a king
     fulfilled in the birth of our salvation
     and she brought forth her firstborn child and wrapped him in swaddling clothes
        and laid him in a manger
     it is through this pain that our salvation is born!

There was stillness on the hillside that night as well
     shepherds watching over the flock by night
     there was a stillness
     perhaps a fire glowing for light and warmth
     perhaps a tiredness that comes from work—hard work over a long day
     now there is stillness—sheep are safely grazing, shepherds resting
     now there is stillness

Until the words of wonder are spoken
     by presence felt—in voice unknown, unknowable
     good tidings of great joy—great joy for all the people
        unto you is born this day a savior who is Christ the Lord
        unto you is born this day salvation and all its splendor
        unto you is born this day a child, wrapped in swaddling clothes and lying in a manger
        unto you is born this day a babe of unwed mother, without power or prestige or position
        unto you is born this day another poor and lowly baby, a child of the no-accounts,
        the nobodies of this world
        unto you is born this day the king of kings and lord of lords
        unto you is born this day the one who shall reign forever and ever
     hallelujah, hallelujah amen

Let us go even unto Bethlehem and see this thing which has come to pass,
     which the Lord hath made known unto us
     in words of wonder, words of faith they proclaimed the deepest desire of the human heart
        to be in the presence of the holy
        to connect with that which is eternal
        to worship God
     and they came and found the child
     they knelt down and they worshiped him

And now the wonder of the ages comes to us
      it is no longer long ago and very far away
      it is no longer about birthing in a manger and shepherds on a hillside
      it is now—it is here—it is us
           in the stillness of this moment God is present
           in the stillness of this moment the child comes—to us.

Christ is born this night—come and worship

Forgiveness is born this night—come and worship
      and at the stable find release from guilt and fear
      find love beyond all measure to make up for all you have done and left undone
           all the ways you have failed
           all the things you could be but haven't yet become

Peace is born this night—come and worship
      and among the lowly animals find a warmth that even warms the soul
      find comfort for your grief, calm in the midst of the trials of your living

Healing is born this night—come and worship
      and in the love that is present here find wholeness for all your brokenness
      find a balm for wounds of the body and torments of the spirit, a salve for every sinsick soul

Joy is born this night—come and worship
      and in the cries that echo forth find not just happiness but something far more precious
      find joy—deep abiding joy that depends not on good times or pleasant circumstances
      find joy that only comes in living as God's own children

Salvation is born this night—come and worship
      and in this manger rude and bare find everything that matters
      find life and love and life made new
      find God, find even God

Christ is born this night—come and worship.

A Family Liturgy for Christmas Day

by Jody Seymour

READER 1: The waiting is over. The time has arrived. A child has come into the darkness to give us light. Each week the light of a candle has illuminated the path of Advent. Now it is time for new birth and new light. This day we are all children ready to unwrap Christmas love.

READER 2: *Read Luke 2:1–16.*

READER 3: Now let's remember the lights along our Advent path.

CHILD: I light this first candle of Advent. Its name is HOPE.

CHILD: I light this second candle of Advent. Its name is LOVE.

CHILD: I light this third candle of Advent. Its name is PEACE.

CHILD: I light this fourth candle of Advent. Its name is JOY.

READER 3: And now it is time for his candle. In the smile of the baby Jesus we see hope, love, peace, and joy. It is time for the light of Christ.

ALL: We light the Christ candle to celebrate the birth of God's special child into our world and into our lives.

READER 4:

O manger child, you smile at us,
A light shines on your brow.
Starlight seems to come your way,
The dark's not so dark now.

Joseph, Mary, bend down low
And whisper in his ear
Our Christmas greeting to your child,
"We're glad that you are here."

Our candles tell the happy news
Of hope, love, peace, and joy.
And now we light a candle bright
To celebrate this boy.

Help us now to tell the world
Christ's light is finally here.
May we go out to spread good news
To all both far and near.

ALL SING: "Go, Tell It on the Mountain"

CHRISTMAS TALES

The Spider's Gift

by Garth House

A S BEAUTIFUL AS A CHRISTMAS TREE IS WITH ITS lights and ornaments, only the silvery tinsel makes the tree truly shimmer and sparkle with light. Even the most scraggly tree can be transformed by shining strands of tinsel. Some people say that we hang tinsel on the Christmas tree to represent icicles. However, another story of why we hang tinsel is one that few people know about.

Almost two thousand years ago, high up in the mountains of Judea in the land of Palestine, there was a road. It wasn't a paved road, or a gravel road, but only a dirt path which climbed steeply up from the valleys of the land of Palestine, over the high mountain passes, and down into the land of Egypt.

At the highest pass this narrow dirt path became very dangerous for travelers. On one side a sharp cliff dropped away for thousands of feet. At the bottom there were sharp rocks and big boulders. On the other side of the dirt path there rose, straight up, a sheer wall of rock so high its top could not be seen. The path was just wide enough for a person and a donkey to get by. Many an unfortunate traveler and beast had fallen on the sharp rocks and big boulders at the bottom of the cliff.

For century after century the wind and rain had beaten against the sheer wall of rock. There were many caves hollowed out of the rock wall. Some of the caves were small, while others were quite large. Many were large enough for travelers to enter. It is in one of these large caves that our story begins.

In this cave high up on a narrow ledge, there lived a tiny black spider. He had been living in the cave for many, many years.

In the morning he would watch the sun rise. He would spin his webs, singing little songs to himself as he spun. At noon he would rest and ponder the deep blue sky, then he would spin some more and sing some more. At evening he would rest again and watch the clouds turn pink, and then orange, and finally deep crimson as the sun sank beneath the horizon. Then came the time the little spider loved best of all. He would sit at the mouth of his cave and watch the stars appear one by one. Finally the moon would rise, and for hours the spider would sit and gaze at the glittering heavens.

Although the little black spider was happy spending his time this way, there was one problem: he was a very lonely spider, for no one had ever come to visit him in all the years he had lived in his cave.

One night the spider was gazing at the heavens when suddenly, in a part of the sky where there had never been a star before, a tiny pinpoint of light appeared. It grew brighter and brighter and brighter, until it was more brilliant than all the other stars in the sky. It was a new star, and blue and white light shot out of it! The little spider was full of wonder and amazement, and thought to himself: "This must be a sign! It must mean that something very special and wonderful is going to happen." He thought and thought, and finally decided that the most wonderful thing that could happen to him would be if someone came to visit him. Full of expectation, he gazed at the new star each night and waited.

Down from the high mountain pass, where the narrow dirt path twisted and snaked its way through the steep mountains, there lay a valley. In the valley there was a town called Bethlehem. In Bethlehem there was an inn and a stable. On the night of our story, the inn was warm and full of light. It was crowded with people who could afford to stay in comfort. The stable, on the other hand, was cold and dark. Inside the stable was a manger, and in the manger lay a brand new baby who was fast asleep. The baby's name was Jesus. On one side of the manger slept his father, Joseph. On the other side slept his mother, Mary.

As Joseph slept, suddenly there appeared to him in a dream an angel of the Lord. The angel's face shone with light. His mighty wings made a great rushing sound and all the colors of the rainbow flashed and danced around him. It was the angel Gabriel. Gabriel said: "Joseph! Joseph! Make haste! Take your Child and your wife and flee to the land of Egypt. Herod, that heartless and wicked king, has sent his soldiers to murder the Child, as well as you and Mary. Quickly, flee to safety, for your family is in great danger!" There was a blinding flash of light, the angel vanished, and Joseph awoke in the darkness of the stable.

Outside the stable he heard the tramping of many feet and the clanging of metal. Terrified, he crept to the door and peered out. Not more than ten feet away, a battalion of Herod's soldiers was marching past, their swords and spears flashing in the moonlight. They were headed toward the inn. Joseph realized there might be time to make an escape.

He touched his sleeping wife. When she awoke he placed a finger to his lips. When Mary saw her husband's face, she knew they were in great danger. Without a word and in great haste they gathered together what few possessions they had. Mary lifted the sleeping Child from the manger. He awoke and began to cry. Mary immediately hugged him to her breast and whispered gentle words to him. Feeling the warmth of his mother's body and the soothing sound of her voice, he fell back to sleep.

Joseph led the donkey out of its stall. He lifted Mary, with the sleeping baby in her arms, up onto the donkey. Taking the donkey by its coarse rope, he led it out of the stable. Quickly and silently they made their way through the back streets of Bethlehem and headed up into the mountains of Judea, taking the road to the land of Egypt.

It was a cold night, and the donkey was a very stubborn donkey. More than once it would set its hooves in the ground, stiffen its legs, and refuse to go any farther. Then Joseph would pull and he would tug until finally the stubborn donkey moved on. In this fashion they made their way slowly up into the mountains.

They had been traveling for many hours. It was well into the night and they had climbed very high. They came to a part of the road that was very dangerous. On the one side a sharp cliff dropped away for thousands of feet, and on the other side there rose, straight up, a sheer wall of rock so high its top could not be seen.

When the donkey saw what lay before him, once again he set his hooves into the ground, stiffened his legs, and refused to move. Joseph pulled and tugged on the rope, but this time he could not get the stubborn beast moving. Then Mary, looking down at her husband, said, "Joseph, look at your hands!" Joseph held up his hands in the moonlight. They were raw and bleeding. Mary said, "Joseph, my husband, you are tired and weary, and I am cold. The donkey will go no farther. Let us go into one of these caves and spend the night. Then, when the sun rises in the morning, we will make our way down into the land of Egypt."

So they found a cave that was large enough even for the donkey. They went into the cave. Joseph lifted Mary, with the Child in her arms, down off the donkey. They lay down on the cold, hard floor of the cave, placed the Child between them, and huddled together for warmth. Soon they were asleep.

Whose cave do you think it was in which they had chosen to spend the night?

When the little black spider heard his guests enter the cave, he was terribly excited. At first he was going to go right down and introduce himself, but then he thought he might frighten his visitors, so he decided to wait.

After a while all was quiet in the cave. The

spider decided to go down and investigate. He spun out a strand of web and lowered himself down from his ledge. Down and down he went until he was suspended right above the sleeping figures on the cave floor. The moonlight flooded in through the mouth of the cave and fell across the sleeping family. The little spider gazed down upon his guests. First he looked on Mary and thought to himself, "Oh, how beautiful she is!" Then he looked on Joseph and thought, "Oh, how kind he is!" But when he beheld the sleeping Child between them, he was filled with great awe and wonder. Somehow the spider knew that here in this Child was something more full of hope than the sun rising in the morning, more peaceful than the sky at noon, more lovely than the clouds at evening, more mysterious and wonderful than even the stars and moon at night. The little spider, hanging there in the cold night air, believed that this Child was going to bring great love and kindness into the world. He hung there, suspended by his web, gazing down in adoration.

Then something unexpected happened. The baby Jesus woke up. He opened his eyes. There in the moonlight above him he saw the little spider dangling from his web. For a moment the spider and the Child looked in astonishment at each other. Then the Child smiled, and then he laughed and reached up with his hand as if to touch the little spider.

When the spider saw that smile and heard that laughter, a joy such as he had never known before flooded through him. In a flash he knew he would never be lonely again, no matter what happened. He knew that the brilliant new star he had seen in the heavens was a sign not just that something wonderful was going to happen to him, but that something wonderful was going to happen to the whole world.

Almost beside himself with joy and excitement, the little spider climbed quickly back to his ledge. He was overcome by a great desire to give a gift to the Child. But, like the baby Jesus, the little spider was very poor. When he looked around his ledge, he saw nothing he could give to his guest. Then he had an idea. "It is very cold in my cave," he said to himself, "but if I spin a web across the mouth of the cave it will keep the wind out. It will grow warm in here for the Child and his parents. Yes, that will be my gift!"

Immediately the little spider set about his task. Up and down he went across the mouth of the cave, spinning his web. Back and forth he went, weaving together intricate patterns of triangles and squares and circles. As he spun, he sang to himself, only now new songs welled up inside him, songs the words and melodies of which he had never thought of before; songs strange and beautiful coming from a place deep inside that he had never known before this night. In great joy and exultation he worked furiously in the moonlight. Finally his work was completed.

This web was the little spider's masterpiece! Never in all the time he had been spinning webs had the spider woven such a splendidly complex and lovely creation. Even the spider himself was amazed at the grandeur and beauty of his work. Very tired, but very happy, he climbed back up to his ledge and fell sound asleep.

Gradually, in the chilly night, ice began to form on the strands of the magnificent web. Before long the whole web was coated with a shining, silver glaze. Like a tapestry of glimmering fire, or a great luminous crystal, the web shone with the reflected light of the moon and stars. The clear white light from the heavens danced off of the ice-covered web in flashes of red and green and royal blue.

For some time there was complete silence, with only the moon and stars as witnesses to the little spider's gift.

Suddenly, down the dirt path, there came the sound of feet tramping on the cold, hard earth. The footsteps came closer and closer to the cave. Mary and Joseph woke up. They heard the footsteps approaching, and then they heard something which put a great fear into their hearts: the harsh, clanging sound of metal swords and spears. Mary and Joseph knew it was Herod's soldiers who approached, and they looked at each other and then at the sleeping Child between them. Tears filled their eyes. They joined hands across the sleeping baby, closed their eyes, and silently offered up a prayer to the God of Israel. They asked God for a miracle that would save them from death at the hands of Herod's men.

The footsteps came closer and closer, until they were right outside the cave. Then there was silence.

Outside the cave stood two of Herod's soldiers.

All night long they had been trudging through the mountains of Judea, going in and out of every cave they came to, looking for the baby Jesus and his parents. They were tired and cold and hungry. Their spirits were heavy, because they did not like the evil mission they had been ordered to carry out.

When they came to the little spider's cave, they stopped. There before them, radiant in the moonlight, was the splendid web. The soldiers stood in great wonder and awe before the web. Never in all their lives had they seen anything so beautiful. For a while neither could speak. Then one of the soldiers, still gazing at the web, whispered to his friend, "Certainly there can be no one in this cave, for if there were this web would be broken." For a moment his friend did not respond. Then, without taking his eyes from the glowing web, he answered in a hushed voice, "You are right. There could be no one here. We should continue our search elsewhere." Yet neither soldier moved. They seemed caught in a spell cast by the beauty of the web.

Finally, the soldier who had spoken first shivered. He remembered the dark errand he had been sent on, and he touched his friend on the shoulder. Reluctantly, the two soldiers moved on and continued their search.

Inside the cave Mary and Joseph heard the footsteps fading away in the distance. They began to weep quietly, not from sadness, but out of joy that God had delivered them and their Child from death.

The baby Jesus and the little black spider had slept soundly through the close brush with Herod's soldiers. Soon Mary and Joseph were also asleep, for the cave had become warm and cozy because of the web spun across the entrance.

So comfortable was the cave, and so tired were its occupants, that for the first time in a long time there was no one at the mouth of the cave in the morning to greet the sun as it rose. By the time Mary and Joseph awoke the rays of the sun had already melted and dissolved the beautiful web.

By the time the spider awoke his guests had already gone on their way to the land of Egypt. But he wasn't sad that his visitors had left. In fact, for the first time in his life, the spider was completely happy. The whole world seemed to be brand new, and the little spider felt that he was just now, for the first time, seeing how really beautiful everything was. He felt like he was brand new also, as though this day was the first day of his life. He sat in the warm sun at the entrance to his cave. A great stillness surrounded him, and in his heart there was peace. He gazed up into the deep blue sky and for the first time in his life, offered up a prayer of thanksgiving for the gift of life.

As for the soldiers? Well, our story is not the last time their paths would cross the life of Jesus of Nazareth. But that is a tale for another time and another place.

What does the story of the little spider's gift have to do with tinsel? Well, this Christmas when you hang the tinsel on the tree, take some strands of it and look at them. Notice how silvery and shiny they are. Then hang them on the tree and see how the different colors from the lights dance and shimmer among the silver strands. Now imagine the beauty of the magnificent web the little spider spun because of his love for Jesus.

We hang tinsel on the tree each Christmas to remind us of the little spider's gift to the Child Jesus. It helps us to remember that giving a gift to someone we love is a wonderful thing, and it can even cause a miracle to happen!

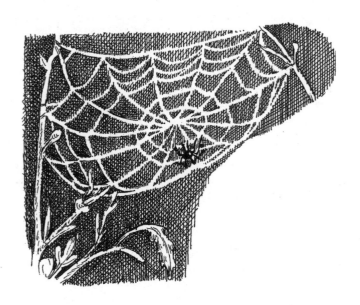

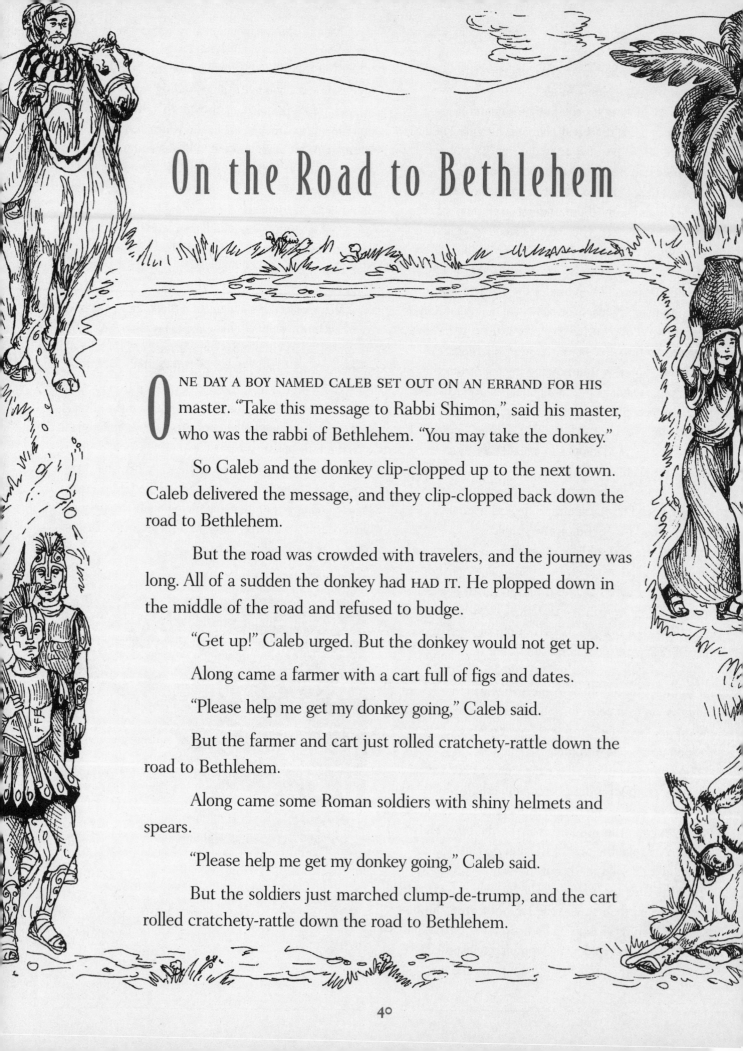

On the Road to Bethlehem

ONE DAY A BOY NAMED CALEB SET OUT ON AN ERRAND FOR HIS master. "Take this message to Rabbi Shimon," said his master, who was the rabbi of Bethlehem. "You may take the donkey."

So Caleb and the donkey clip-clopped up to the next town. Caleb delivered the message, and they clip-clopped back down the road to Bethlehem.

But the road was crowded with travelers, and the journey was long. All of a sudden the donkey had HAD IT. He plopped down in the middle of the road and refused to budge.

"Get up!" Caleb urged. But the donkey would not get up.

Along came a farmer with a cart full of figs and dates.

"Please help me get my donkey going," Caleb said.

But the farmer and cart just rolled cratchety-rattle down the road to Bethlehem.

Along came some Roman soldiers with shiny helmets and spears.

"Please help me get my donkey going," Caleb said.

But the soldiers just marched clump-de-trump, and the cart rolled cratchety-rattle down the road to Bethlehem.

Along came a rich merchant riding a proud camel.

"Please help me get my donkey going," Caleb said.

But the merchant just shouted, "Make way!" and the soldiers marched clump-de-trump and the cart rolled cratchety-rattle down the road to Bethlehem.

Along came a servant girl carrying a heavy jar of water.

"Please help me get my donkey going," Caleb said.

But the servant girl just went slosh-swash and the merchant shouted, "Make way!" and the soldiers marched clump-de-trump and the cart rolled cratchety-rattle down the road to Bethlehem.

By now the sun had set and the sky was getting dark. Still the donkey would not get up.

All of a sudden, high in the sky ahead, a brilliant light sparkled. It was a star. But what a star it was! Caleb had never seen anything like it.

"Look!" he told the donkey.

The donkey gave a great "**hee–haw!**" He jumped to his hooves and clippity-clopped down the road as fast as he could. Caleb hung on tightly to the donkey's stubby mane.

Along the way they saw the servant girl going slosh-swash and the merchant shouting, "Make way!" and the soldiers marching clump-de-trump and the cart rolling cratchety-rattle while the donkey galloped clippity-clop and the star shone . . .

and the star shone . . .

and the star shone . . .

all on the road to Bethlehem.

The Last Child in Line

by William D. Kennedy

To the weary, bloodshot eyes of Ned Gruber, the seasonal Santa impersonator at the Yellow Springs Mall, the most wonderful sight came at nine o'clock on December 24th. That's when they finally extinguished the glaring blink of red and green lights around the "Santa's Village" display in front of Quincy's department store. Each night during the holiday season, Santa's two oversized "elves," who bore an uncanny resemblance to the uninspired students in Ned's history classes at Yellow Springs High, waited for the dimming lights to signal the time to pull the silver tasseled cord across the back of the line of children waiting to have their photo taken with Saint Nick. So far this year, more than eight hundred children had climbed atop Ned's lap in just forty days, each with their own secret wishes and dreams for Christmas morning.

Ned considered himself lucky if by nine o'clock there were only a handful more children left in line. If so, he might have time to slip into the "Santa's Workshop" facade to change his clothes before the mall closed its doors at nine thirty. More often than not, however, Ned found that those last kids, unpressured by any significant backlog behind them, took much more time per child than those earlier in the day, and he'd still be sitting on his Santa throne well past closing time. Tonight seemed to be no different. As the fifty-third child of the day slid from his padded knees, Ned glanced over his artificial half-glasses to see how many more visitors remained. The line curved away from his view, which meant at least eight or nine more.

With a tired sigh, Ned nodded to an elf, indicating it was all right to let the next child come forward. The frightened little boy—he couldn't be more than three, Ned figured—was practically dragged up to Santa, screaming and crying the whole way. His visit was just long enough for the flash of the instant print camera. As the frustrated father led away his tearful son, Ned made an instinctive retreat into the "Workshop" and grabbed the flask of liquid courage he always kept nearby. He raised it toward his lips, then stopped. "No," he thought, "I promised myself I could make it through the week without any 'Christmas Cheer,' and I've come too far to give up now."

When Ned took the Santa job four Christmases ago, things were different. That first year, he was actually disappointed when the last child passed off his lap. Back then, he worked to earn some extra spending money for his wife and infant daughter. But in the next year, Ned found himself living alone in a one-room efficiency above the Crow's Nest Pub after two disastrous affairs. The first was with the new English teacher who had a homeroom across from his; it lasted only until his wife and girlfriend found out about each other. The second was with the bottle; it began shortly after the first affair ended, and had continued until just four days ago.

From that time on, Ned's seasonal role as Saint Nick was a way to keep him from the loneliness of a bar stool during the holidays. After he surrendered his visitation rights, he had hoped his wife might bring their daughter to visit Santa. That first year after she changed the locks on him, he actually saw her in line,

but his wife must have learned who was behind the white beard, because the little girl had never made it to his lap. Given how poorly he had treated his wife, Ned didn't really blame her. Since then, playing Santa let him see joy and excitement in a child's eyes, none of which he had seen since he last laid eyes on his three-month-old baby.

A six-year-old boy named Dwight was next in line. After climbing onto Santa's red corduroy lap, he demanded to know if that was really him at the Thanksgiving Parade and, if so, why hadn't he waved back at him? Ned was used to this type of cross-examination by now. In fact, he had heard just about every imaginable question pop from the mouths of doubting children, and he prided himself on smart, persuasive answers.

"Yes, Dwight, that was me, all right. I was looking at you earlier, while you were watching the float in front of Santa. Santa always wants to say hello to all the good boys and girls. Now, what would you like me to bring you tomorrow morning?"

Ned had found that a deft redirection of the conversation towards "presents" almost always worked. He would then lean down towards the child conspiratorially, nodding with feigned interest, as if he were memorizing the wish list. At the same time, a small microphone tucked under his artificial beard carried the child's secrets to his parents, who listened in on a small earphone over by the exit from Santa's Village. The electronics had been Ned's innovation a few years ago. He had found that some kids would only reveal their wishes to Santa, and when parents approached him later, he was rarely able to remember which child had asked for what. Allowing parents to eavesdrop made him the most popular Santa in the whole area, a fact which the mall did not overlook in his paycheck.

After Dwight was a girl, a little older than many, who had her faith in Santa shaken when she found the microphone hidden in his whiskers as she hugged him, but Ned was ready for her. "Sweetie," he explained, "Santa is very old, and he doesn't hear so well anymore. This little thing is a special kind of hearing aid that helps Santa hear your secrets better."

The girl considered this, found it logical, then began to confide her own special Christmas dreams.

Ned had found that children had grown smarter over the past few years. The next child had heard that Santa was at Pepper's Discount Mart, and wanted to know how he could be in two places at one time.

"Well," Ned began, "Santa is everywhere—all the time! That's how I can 'see you when you're sleeping' and 'know when you're awake'! Even when you can't see me, I can see you!" That, followed by a question about presents, had ended the inquiry.

The following child was borderline non-believer. She accused him of being a fake. Her big brother said there was no such thing as Santa. Ned demurred to these "coming-of-age" confrontations. "Well, sometimes people believe things in a different way when they get older. But maybe ol' Santa can prove himself to you. How about if I tell you now, right here, about something special I'll leave for you. Not anything big, mind you—that would make your big brother jealous—but something that you and I will know is a special sign that I'm as real as you want me to be." Then he suggested that their special sign would be a shiny red apple in her stocking. Ned knew that his microphone system was working when children would come back the next year and thank him for leaving the special apple.

After that came a belligerent eight-year-old who demanded to know why he hadn't gotten everything he asked for last year. Ned responded with a brief interrogation about his behavior over the previous

months, gently pointing out the need for improvement, but assuring him that there would be pleasant surprises under the tree this year. The next child wanted to know how come presents from Santa came in boxes from the people who made things for the toy stores. For that, Ned pulled out his explanation about how there were so many good boys and girls that the elves at the North Pole couldn't make enough toys, and so they hired other companies to help.

As an unusually chunky lad tumbled off Ned's lap, he glanced at the clock and saw it was almost nine thirty. One of his elves, slumping against the camera tripod, held up one finger, indicating there was only one more to go. The mall lights were already being dimmed, and Ned could see shoppers filing past the guards at the door. His back was sore, his shirt was sweat drenched, and his knees ached as one final believer approached him, hesitantly, but on her own. Despite his weariness, Ned felt a strange sadness at this moment. After this there would be no more kicked shins, no more drool on his cheek, no more ear-splitting wails, and no more pulling at the beard he had spirit-gummed to his face. It also meant no more cuddling with happy children, no more smiles, no more squeals of delightful ecstasy as a little one saw Santa in the flesh for the first time.

Ned summoned his last burst of Christmas enthusiasm for the little girl he hoisted onto his lap. Four, maybe five years old, he estimated. "Hello, sweetie! Merry Christmas. I know *you've* been a good girl this year, haven't you?"

She giggled coyly. "Uh huh."

"Good! Now, tell me, what can Santa bring to your house for Christmas?"

The little girl smiled confidently at him, as if he already knew what she would ask for. "If I tell you, you have to promise to bring it, okay?"

Ned had heard this one before. "Well, Santa will do his best, but I can't promise anything. That's against the rules. What is it you want to see tomorrow morning?"

"My daddy," she said.

The request startled Ned. He had heard a lot of kids ask for a lot of unusual things, from world peace to a baby bunny rabbit instead of a baby brother or sister, but he had never been asked to produce a father before.

"What's that, honey?" Ned feigned being hard of hearing while he thought about how to proceed.

"I said," she repeated with the patience of a schoolteacher to a daydreaming pupil, "I want you to bring me my daddy for Christmas."

"Tell me, sweetie, where is your daddy?"

The child just giggled, as if she were too smart to fall for Santa's trick. "*You* know! You're Santa!"

Ned laughed along with her, chuckling his best ho-ho-ho of the season. "Oh, but it's late, my dear, and I've been thinking about all the presents I'm going to bring you. Can't you remind ol' Santa where your daddy is?"

"Mommy says he lives in a Special Place where they don't let kids."

Ned quickly considered the possibilities. The "Special Place" sounded like either the military or prison. No, not the military—the mother would be proud of that, and the girl would probably know where her old man was stationed. It had to be prison.

"Well, honey, Santa will see what he can do, but sometimes people have to stay in the Special Place for a long time. I don't know if I can get your daddy out so soon."

The smile on the little girl's face never faded. "Yes, you can! You're *Santa Claus!*"

If he weren't so worried about how to let this child down without disappointing her, Ned would have been amazed by the girl's limitless faith. Instead, he tried to steer her to safer pastures. "Well, what else would you like for Christmas? Maybe there's something *special* that I can leave in a hiding place that only you and I know about."

That line had nearly always worked. The child would confide about a secret spot—like under a chair or behind a curtain—and the microphone would carry the message to the parent who would see to it that a particular gift would be there on Christmas morning. Ned figured a trick like that was good for extending the onset of disbelief by at least a year.

But it didn't work on this little girl. "I don't want anything else. Just Daddy. Last night when I said my prayers, I asked Jesus for Daddy, and now I'm asking you."

Great, thought Ned, just great. The kid's faith in both Santa and God was tied to a prisoner's release at Christmas. He leaned forward in the chair, trying to see over to where the mother would be listening in on this conversation. Maybe the mother would give him a signal to let him know whether he should promise something. Ned strained his eyes, staring into the darkening mall, but the little girl blocked his view of the exit where Mom would be. Still, Ned knew that someone had to be listening in on their conversation, so he asked, "Now, when you said your prayers last night, and when you asked Jesus for your daddy, was your mommy there with you?" Come on, lady, he thought, give me some help here.

"Yes, sir," the girl answered with a seriousness that reflected her understanding that prayer was a mature, grown-up activity. "And Mommy said that if I asked Jesus, and if I came here tonight and asked you, my daddy would come home for Christmas."

Bingo! thought Ned. Now we've got it! Wherever this kid's dad is, the mom wouldn't have risked destroying her daughter's innocent faith unless she was pretty darn sure the old man would show.

"Is that right, sweetie? That's what your mommy said?" He looked over the girl's shoulder toward where the mother had to have been standing, hoping for a confirming nod or something.

At first he saw no one, but then he saw movement in the shadows. Then the dim light caught her anxious, almost frightened expression. Ned's heart jumped and a shiver jolted his spine. If she was the mother, then he was the father of the girl in his lap.

In a cracking voice, Ned repeated, "You're sure that's what your mommy said?"

The woman—his wife—looked at him hard, her eyes glued to his, then nodded. She would let him come home. She *wanted* him to come home!

Ned felt lightheaded and slumped back in his chair. The girl on his lap was no longer visitor number eight hundred eighty-nine, but rather was Emily Sarah Gruber, named after his own grandmother. He could see it now—his wife's soft, gentle chin and sharp blue eyes. Tears filled his eyes and ran down his beard as he hugged his daughter tightly. He buried her head in his shoulder.

The little girl seemed confused, but she hugged Ned back anyhow. "Santa, what's the matter? What are you sorry for?"

He hadn't even realized that he had spoken his apology out loud. He released his grip and sniffed hard, trying to resume his role. "Oh, Emily, dear sweet Emily, Santa is just so very, very sorry that he didn't bring your daddy home sooner. Your daddy will be there tomorrow morning."

Emily's eyes widened. "He will?!? You promise?!?"

Ned nodded. "I promise. You can tell your mommy that Santa said so."

Emily threw her little arms around him as tight as she could. "Oh, thank you, Santa! Thank you! I just knew you could do it!"

Ned kissed the girl's head. "But you have to do Santa a favor," he told her. "Thank your mother, too. And tonight, when you say your prayers? I want you to thank Jesus for me, too, will you? Those two have more to do with your daddy coming back than ol' Santa."

Emily vowed she would do just that. She flew off his knee, calling excitedly to her mommy. Ned watched as his daughter told his wife all about Santa's promise. Ned wanted to call her then, but he was too choked up to speak. His wife handed something to Emily, who ran back towards him, cutting under the felt ropes that lined the exit.

"Here, Santa. This is for you, from my mom." She handed him a little red box, then leaned up and kissed her father on his cheek. As she ran away again, Ned pulled the ribbon and opened the package. Inside was a shiny new brass door key. A note read:

'For God so loved the world that he gave his only begotten Son that whoever would believe in him would not perish, but have everlasting life' (John 3:16). Christmas is for new beginnings. Please come home."

Ned rose from his Santa's chair, but by then, his wife and daughter were gone, lost in the crowd of exiting shoppers.

"Hey, Santa," one of his elves called to him, "we're done here. Don't you have somewhere you ought to be going?"

"Yes," Ned replied quietly. "I'm going home."

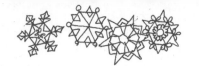
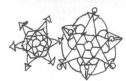
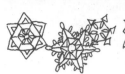

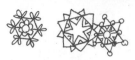

Christmas Eve with Ivan

by Arthur F. Fogartie

SNOW! THIS IS NEAT—THIS IS PERFECT! DON'T LIKE it any other time. Makes it too wet. But Christmas Eve needs it. Snow!

Needs lots of things, Christmas Eve, I mean. Like peace on earth . . . and reindeer . . . and good will . . . and angels . . . and presents. A shepherd would be nice. No wise men, though. They didn't come 'til later. Ivan knows the story.

From the East, they were. East . . . Asia . . . dark, strange men from dark, strange places bringing dark, strange gifts. Burial ointments for the Baby. Yichh!

Ivan was a wise man once. No, not in the play. Ivan was the littlest shepherd boy in the church play. No, Ivan was a wise man. Lots of money. Lots of friends. Lots of things. *Let's do lunch . . . . Tennis later? About two-ish? . . . Ciao, babe.*

They came from all over to hear the wise man: *Better not do that now—bad timing . . . Invest over here . . . Double production there . . . Broaden this . . . Eliminate that.* Yeah! They all raised their eyebrows and stroked their chins. Ivan, the wise man.

Yep, that's what we need—snow. Christmas Eve needs snow and other stuff. Ivan needs new shoes. Wet goes right through the cardboard. But—gotta have snow on Christmas Eve.

Bundle up the Baby, Mother Mary. Angels make him smile, but blankets keep him warm. Always watch the Baby. Babies need lots of help.

Snow—good snow—white and fluffy and dry. That'll keep Ivan's feet un-wet. Didn't have any good shoes for Ivan at the shelter. Maybe New Year's. Folks'll get rid of their old shoes when Santa brings them new ones. Ivan will make it.

Ivan is Ivan because of Caesar, you know. Caesar called himself Caesar. Learned that in eighth grade—Mr. Spurrier's history. Sat next to Ricky . . . Ricky . . . Ricky Walker. Smart boy. Ivan spent the night with Ricky once during Christmas break. No tree, no stockings, no peppermint. Ricky was poor. Wore bad clothes—jacket with a hole in it. Poor . . . and happy.

Ivan ate dinner with them, and, after, they all sang. Took turns. They even made Ivan sing. Mrs. Walker had a wonderful voice. She sang "Sweet Little Jesus Boy." Hers was best. Ivan cried.

> *. . . born in a manger.*
> *Sweet little holy child,*
> *Didn't know who you wuz.*

We don't have many decorations, she told Ivan, *but we've got each other and we've got the Baby Lord, and he always comes when we need him. That's enough.*

Ricky Walker . . . history class . . . Caesar was Caesar. Ivan remembered when Ivan got rich.

"Merry Christmas!" Ivan knows him. Works in Ivan's bank . . . used to be Ivan's bank. "Yes, sir! No, sir! I'm sorry, sir! More coffee, sir? Merry Christmas, sir!" Oh, they treated Ivan fine. Ivan was a wise man.

Now Ivan mostly sees the guards. They're nice. Ivan was always nice to them—tall, straight guards in blue suits. . .

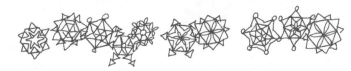

. . . Mother Mary wore a blue dress, you know. Blue chiffon. matched her eyes . . .

. . . Tommy had blue eyes—green and blue. They changed, dark and flashing. Ivan remembers the poem:

> *Those eyes the greenest of things blue,*
> *The bluest of things grey.*
> *Eyes colored like a water-flower,*
> *And deeper than the green sea's glass.*
>
> *Eyes that remember one sweet hour—*
> *In vain we swore it should not pass.*

Look into the Baby's eyes, Mother Mary. Look deep and hold on. They get sick, you know. They get sick, and weak, and inoperable, and they fade away. Far, far away.

Ivan's bank! The big one over there—built forty-five stories tall with Ivan's money. Ivan was a mover and a shaker. Ivan was a wise man. Caesar was Caesar. Ivan is Ivan. Ivan lived the poem:

> *It matters not how strait the gate,*
> *How charged with punishments the scroll,*
> *I am the master of my fate;*
> *I am the captain of my soul.*

All roads lead to Ivan. Take it to Ivan, he can solve it. No problem too tough for Ivan. *And Ivan will reign until he has put all enemies under his feet. And the last enemy to be destroyed is . . . Death.*

Not destroyed yet, you know. The Man with the Sickle is still out there. One at a time, he gets them all. He got Caesar. He got Mother Mary. He got Tommy.

> *And all the King's horses*
> *and all the King's men*
> *Couldn't put Humpty-Dumpty together again.*

That's right, Tommy. Very, very good. You learned that one fast. Let's hear another. You're so smart. Good boy. How about a catch? What to throw with your old dad? Okay, burn it in. No, no! That's low minors stuff. It's outta here! Over the fence! A one-way bus ticket back home! Bring some heat!

Atta boy! That's your good stuff. Mow 'em down. Fourteen in a row. Way to go, Tommy! That's my kid out there. Seven-oh this year. Unhittable! Pitched the winning game in the high school state championship last year.

Look! Look over there—the guy in the hat! Yeah, the one with the clipboard. Scout for the pros. Wants to talk to Tommy right after the game. They're gonna offer him a contract because he's . . . the best . . . they've ever . . . seen.

> *Buy me some peanuts and Cracker Jack.*
> *I don't care if I ever get back.*

No more baseball.
No more pro scouts.
No more Tommy.

What do you mean, inoperable? Fix it! You transplant hearts, for God's sake. Do something. Help him. He's seventeen years old, for cryin' out loud! He's still got games to pitch . . . and hearts to break . . . and malls to . . .

. . . Ivan went to the mall the other day. Yes, Ivan goes to the mall. Ivan loves to look. No touching! Never touch! If Ivan touches, they think Ivan steals. Never, never touch!

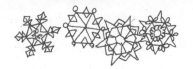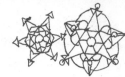

So many pretty things. Little dolls dressed like elves . . . Santa with a long line at his cardboard North Pole house . . . excited children, running and laughing and pointing and asking . . . wonderful children. It's a happy time.

> *Christmas is coming, the goose is getting fat.*
> *Please put a penny in the old man's hat.*
> *If you don't have a penny, a half-a-cent will do.*
> *If you don't have a half-a-cent, God bless you!*

Excited children . . . and angry parents. Why are they angry? Ivan even saw a woman slap her son. Slap! At Christmas! "Pow"—right on the head.

Ivan doesn't speak to strangers—scares them. But Ivan spoke to the slapping lady.

Mother Mary didn't hit her boy. She wouldn't hit the Baby. The Baby's coming. Don't hit your boy or the Baby can't bring him to see you. Ivan never hit Tommy. Tommy comes.

Love that boy, lady. Love him tight. Squeeze all his love 'til it runs out. I loved Tommy 'til there wasn't any left. Christmas is not for hitting, lady. Christmas is for love.

Ivan told her that 'cause Ivan knows the poem:

> *Love came down at Christmas,*
> *Love all lovely, Love divine;*
> *Love was born at Christmas,*
> *Star and Angels gave the sign.*

The Security Man asked Ivan to leave. He was nice. He knows Ivan. Ivan just scares people sometimes.

You like Ivan's shirt? It's new. Got it the same place as last year—at the Big Church. Ivan didn't used to go there. Not close enough to Ivan's big house. Now Ivan lives downtown at the shelter, so Ivan goes to the Big Church.

Here's the Church . . .
. . . here's the steeple.

It has a big steeple—a huge, iron finger that points to the Baby. It shows us where to look. On the lawn of the Big Church they have a stable. Mother Mary . . . Joseph . . . and the Baby in a box. Little Baby. Ivan guards the Baby. Ivan keeps him safe 'til the shepherds come to watch.

The Big Church feeds Ivan breakfast on the Sunday before Christmas—Ivan and two or three hundred of Ivan's friends. We all come in. It smells terrible—like a zoo . . .

> *The rhino is a homely beast.*
> *For human eyes he's not a feast.*
> *Farewell, farewell, you old rhinoceros,*
> *I'll look at something less preposeros.*

Isn't that a funny poem, Tommy? Let's go look at the elephants. There's a silly poem about them, too . . .

Anyway, Ivan and his friends make the Big Church smell bad, but the people there are nice. They give Ivan soap, and a toothbrush, and a comb, and a shirt. Every year! It's soft because it's new.

And red! See? Red checks! Ivan's favorite. Bright, like Tommy's fireman's hat with the siren and the light on top. He ran all over the house on Christmas Day with the light blinding everyone and the woo-woo-woo all day. Ivan finally took out the batteries. Told Tommy it was broken until later. Ivan hated the red fireman's hat. Now Ivan misses it.

See Ivan's red shirt? It's so pretty Ivan put it on right then. Ivan went into the bathroom and changed. Ivan just threw the other one away. A whole year makes a shirt not soft anymore.

Ivan likes the manger scene at the Big Church. Mary's so pretty, and Joseph's so strong. But Ivan really likes the Baby. He's Ivan's special friend. Ivan stays with the Baby tonight—not at the shelter like usual. Ivan lets someone else have Ivan's place. On Christmas Eve, Ivan stays with the Baby.

The police who watch the Big Church used to try to run Ivan off—"Get out of there!"—but Ivan explained it all, and now they understand and check on Ivan.

Don't cry for Ivan. Not tonight. It's Christmas Eve. It's Jingle Bells and Rudolph. It's angels and little lambs.

Don't cry for Ivan. This is the best night of all. Tonight we all stay in the stable. The Baby . . . Ivan . . . and Tommy.

Tonight, Ivan sees the Child—both of them.

CHRISTMAS REFLECTIONS

A Bethlehem Advent

by Israel Galindo

OUR TOUR BUS ENTERS INTO THE "MODERN DAY" city of Bethlehem, just six miles southwest of Jerusalem. After years of mental images associating this small town with Christmas, Magi, and angels, the reality is a disappointment. Bethlehem today is a small Arab town—Arabs being among the poor minority of Jerusalem. If it had a twin sister city in our state, we'd call it "a hole in the wall" kind of place. Aside from the tourist-trap shops and the unlikely predominance of obnoxious street vendors, there is no real hint that anything interesting exists in this dusty little town.

Even the center of attraction, the Church of the Nativity, isn't much to look at. At least not by the standards of the typical western tourist who is used to being entertained and "wowed" by the usual vacation attractions. Bethlehem is no theme park! No amusement rides here, no attractions, no courtesy stations, and no telling when most of the grayish buildings last had a good paint job.

We're ushered into the Church of the Nativity like so much cattle. "Stay together!" yells the tour guide, squelching any rising feeling of devotion the more pious among us may muster. By this time I'm wishing I were back in the City of David—at least there one can gape at the majesty of the Dome of the Rock, one of the most beautiful buildings in the world.

We mill around the church, staring with little interest at nameless icons and buying candles to be lit by the local priest for a blessing. We're waiting for another tour group to vacate the lower section of the church, where the "real attraction" is.

I turn from examining an ancient icon of the Madonna and Child to see my dad in friendly conversation with the priest. I laugh to myself at the sight of my seventy-five-year-old father, who speaks only broken English, talking with a Russian Orthodox priest.

"What on earth can they be talking about?" I wonder. "How can they possibly be talking about anything?" But they laugh together, pull at each other's beards, and hug each other. One of our group snaps their picture: two bearded, rotund, jolly men, a glint of mischief in their eyes, hamming it up for the camera—both looking like candidates for the J.C. Penney Santa Claus kiddy stand. What a sight!

We're finally ushered down the ancient stone stairs and we form a half-circle around the tour guide who, in practiced reverential tones, recounts the significance of this site: before us stands the traditional manger where the Christ Child was born. Off to the side, on the floor, burns an eternal flame within a silver plate in the shape of the Star of Bethlehem. This marks "the exact spot where the Savior was born."

My response is less than spiritual. "Oh, yeah?" I

mutter to myself. "How do you know this is the 'exact' spot?" I'm surprised by my cynicism in this holy place. Aching feet and thirst are not conducive to being spiritually receptive, I conclude.

Some from our group go upstairs to the gift shop, and the crowd thins. I find myself before the silver star, staring into the flame. I forget my aching feet and, wondering timidly, "Could this really be the place where he was born?" I am overcome with awe at the mystery of Spirit turned to flesh in the body of an adolescent girl. My mind gropes to understand how the Ultimate can be contained in an embryo of tissue and bone and blood. I am moved to tears to think of Infinite Love giving movement and breath to the soft body of a baby—warm, innocent, fragile, finite. I am overwhelmed with the sudden realization of the meaning of Advent: waiting in hope for the Divine to enter our lives.

All of a sudden it doesn't matter whether this is really the spot. It doesn't matter that this isn't the "original" silver Star of Bethlehem. (The church has been looted three times.) None of it matters in the presence of such Truth: God has come in the flesh. Emmanuel! He has become flesh with us that we might become spirit with him.

The miracle is still here in this holy place: in pilgrims who come to celebrate the mystery; in the faith that can believe in spite of disappointment; in the divine love that dwells in our imperfect hearts. And in two old men—strangers from halfway around the world—who meet on holy ground and embrace like brothers and laugh in unrestrained joy. Emmanuel!

Jesus' Birthday at Our House

by Ella Pearson Mitchell and Henry H. Mitchell

I S IT POSSIBLE TO RETURN CHRISTMAS TO THE REAL "reason for the season"? Our retail sales system, with its heavy dependence on Christmas shopping, will not yield to half-hearted measures. It is our belief that the answer will come a family at a time, followed by whole congregations, and ultimately by a sweeping, contagious countercultural movement of nationwide proportions.

We faced this challenge as a family nearly fifty years ago, as our first child approached his second Christmas. We quietly decided that it was Jesus' birthday, and no matter what other families were doing, we would give all of our presents to Jesus, or to "the least of these." The concrete criterion for validating our choices of gifts was that those to whom we gave could not possibly give presents to us in return, and the gifts had to be relevant to their real needs.

As the children grew, their involvement in the presents-for-Jesus project grew. Their excitement in sending breeder rabbits to Ecuador (through Church World Services) made for a really merry Christmas for Jesus' birthday. The later reports on the rabbit population sustained their interest and rewarded their efforts. Meanwhile, each child knew that we would be just as generous and careful in choosing presents when her or his own birthday came around, each in a different quarter of the year.

The choices of presents for Jesus covered a wide range. There was a Christmas when we sent blankets to an African country, again through Church World Service. We had to learn more about Africa to understand why blankets were needed. We had thought it would be too hot ever to need covers of any kind. Another year we gave Braille story books for blind children, through the John Milton Society. As the children matured and their interests broadened, we sent a $500 check to the Southern Christian Leadership Conference one year. Whatever the project, the choice was made by family vote during our "Together Time."

There were a few projects in which there was more direct personal contact. One Christmas we went to nearby Auberry Indian Mission and brought to our home an orphaned teenager, recommended by the Pattens, American Baptist missionaries. He stayed with us two weeks and received all of the presents. Our church's youth took him to their hearts, and the only downside to it all was the tearful farewell when he had to return.

Of course, the most important Christmas of all was announced thus in the annual family communiqué: "Unto us a son is given." That was the year we voted to adopt a four-year-old Korean "war orphan" named Kim (now legally Ken) through the International Social Service. The rule for his presents was that they had to be useful. The most exciting gift

was a pedal-pumped airplane won by big brother Hank on a children's show.

This self-sufficient, countercultural family group did have second thoughts about gifts, however. One year when the children were in their teens, we voted to appropriate $200; task forces were chosen to select and purchase a Christmas present for each member of the family. On the first shopping expedition, they were disgusted by the crush of crowds and the prices of gifts. To make matters worse, they were deeply disappointed with the rather useless choices they had to make. The most expensive present of all was an exercise machine for Mommy, which she used only a few times. To put it bluntly, we never, ever again heard any requests for a typical American gift-exchange Christmas.

After fifty-one years of marriage, we are still observing Jesus' birthday "our way." Grandchildren are treated as were their parents, at Christmas and on their own birthdays. And our most meaningful Christmas gatherings as a tribe center around the beautiful music of Christmas and our joyous efforts to sing it in four parts.

May the peace and joy of Christmas be yours, this year and every day.

In the Spirit of Giving

by Lee Hill-Nelson

BUD PUGH, YOUTH DIRECTOR OF A CHURCH IN western Colorado, looked out his window at the falling snow. It was two weeks before Thanksgiving. Bud thought about how much the out-of-doors already looked like Christmas while he pondered a project for his youth group. An idea had been building in his mind for some time. He wanted to plan a way for the teenagers to be with someone other than peers and do something to make a difference in another person's Christmas. In this area of the country there was unemployment due to the oil crisis, and Bud's was not a monied church.

"Perhaps the community would like to help us," he thought. He began to work on a plan.

The next day was Saturday. He and twenty-five youth gathered together and visited six nursing homes. At each place they talked with a nursing home worker and got names of residents who had no family or had been abandoned by families. There were ninety-seven residents who had no one visiting them.

On Sunday after church, the youth group met again in the parking lot of the church and divided into groups. This time they were to visit and ask each resident of the nursing homes what he or she wanted for Christmas.

Some of the elderly persons were too feeble to communicate, but a worker gave the youth a list of things that they needed. Others were so excited to have young visitors, and wanted to talk so much, it was hard for them to think about Christmas. Their wants were simple, almost childlike.

"All I want is an apple pie," said one woman.

Others asked for bath powder, shaving lotion, socks, candy, coffee mugs, puzzles, a mirror. One man wanted a John Elway poster and T-shirt.

On Thursday a list of names with 220 desired gifts was printed in the local newspaper asking anyone who wished to donate to the program. Immediately gifts began to arrive, and by Monday, 198 had been brought to the church office. In all, 350 gifts, plus money, were donated. One woman in Evanston, Illinois, sent money after she heard about the project from friends in Colorado.

Again, just before Christmas, the teenagers and youth director went to the nursing homes, this time with wrapped gifts. Excitement built as the teens went from room to room playing Santa Claus. Some of the elderly recipients cried when they were given their gifts. One woman said, "I just don't believe that is for me. No one's given me a gift in a long time." Others in their feebleness did not talk, but there was a gleam in their eyes.

The teens learned much about older people. Some visits were happy. In their get-acquainted time, the youth learned that elderly people had had some of the same experiences they were now having as they

listened to tales of the "good old days."

"A guy ninety years old is like us—not immature, just youthful," said one young man.

Other visits were sad. A girl said, "I wonder why their children don't want them to be a part of their lives anymore. It's like putting an old bicycle away in a garage."

Friendships were begun. Promises were made to return again. There was laughter where there had been no laughter for a long time.

"This project will continue on a monthly basis," said Bud Pugh. "We won't stop now. We've gotten something good started, good for our youth and good for the nursing home residents."

I was a part of the community that donated gifts. I asked my husband to give me the amount of money he was planning to spend for me.

"The nursing home gifts will be your present to me," I told him.

As I wrapped my gifts, I knew the feeling of joy—that it really is more blessed to give than to receive.

Yet I received. As I read the newspaper account of the project and the happiness generated by these young people, and knew that visits would continue, I was thrilled to have been a small part of the project.

"If there are ninety-seven people in this area without loved ones, how many more across the United States must be alone at Christmas?" I asked my husband.

I had everything I needed. What I gave was small for me but big to the ones who received.

Because of one man's vision, Christmas was happier for the givers as well as for the receivers.

Put Christ Back into Christmas?

by Jody Seymour

I T'S HARD TO PUT SOMETHING BACK THAT WAS NEVER there to begin with. I remember the first time I heard the rejection of the effort to put Christ back into Christmas. It came from a preacher years ago who was preaching to a bunch of seminary students. I was one of those students. It was Advent, and exams surrounded us like so much wilderness. We all had Christmas shopping to do, but first theological answers had to be given to expectant professors who seemed to resemble various forms of the Grinch.

And here was a diminutive preacher screaming at a bunch of would-be ministers to "quit beating people up about putting Christ back into Christmas." He told us to cease and desist from guilt-dripping sermons about the "reason for the season." He then did a bit of history about the dating of Christmas and informed us that the celebration of Christmas was a very human custom invented by a distant pope who wanted to keep Christians from such pagan rituals as the Roman Saturnalia festival and the various nature cults that held celebrations around the winter solstice.

The ranting preacher then showed us that according to scriptural evidence, we have no idea when Jesus was born, and in fact it would probably have been in spring rather than winter, since the language used about "shepherds keeping watch over their flocks by night" seemed to refer to a warm-weather condition. In other words, Jesus was not in Christmas to begin with.

The earliest celebrations of Christmas involved remembering Jesus' baptism and the miracle at Cana. It seemed that early Christianity was more interested in who the man was than how he got here. Could it be that we have lapsed into needing stories of a virgin birth and angels' songs because "who he was" is troublesome in terms of our lifestyle issues? The grown-up Jesus asks some not-so-childlike behaviors of those who wish to follow him, like being careful not to let money rule our lives, and giving it away rather than spending it at the malls in order to complete Christmas list obligations.

History will show, the preacher concluded, that the date of Christ's birth was chosen so that Christianity could compete with pagan ritual. But we have lost that competition, chided the preacher. We should give up, enjoy family time, and celebrate the "real" Christmas on January 6 which is Epiphany, sometimes called "old Christmas." It is an option, I suppose.

Perhaps the real parable of the problem is that in the midst of all the created business of the season, Christ still comes. The date does not matter. The historical truth is that the night, whenever it was, was not so silent. Bethlehem was noisy and crowded. The neon sign over the inn buzzed "no vacancy." Mary screamed and groaned like any woman in labor. Unlike the fantasy Christmas carol we love to sing, the "little Lord Jesus" did cry, because human babies must.

Bethlehem might as well have been a parking lot with no parking space in sight. It might as well have been a long checkout line. Angry people who could not find anymore "Tickle Me Elmos" or whatever is the latest must-have toy of the season could have formed a perfect backdrop for his almost unnoticed birth in the midst of the "pagan" rituals we seem always to observe.

Put Christ back into Christmas? He may be puzzled at our efforts to do so, since he was not there to begin with. God still picks the time, and often that time is when we least expect the appearance of God's grace. Incarnation is God's doing. Emmanuel still means "God with us." So pick a day and it could be Christmas.

For now, the only silent night that can be had in the midst of the craziness we call Christmas is the silent night we choose to observe. We cannot wait for it to be still; we must make it still. The frenzy, the greed, the misplaced priorities will not stop, just as the world did not stop that night, whenever it was, long

ago when Christmas happened on God's time. God simply goes ahead with birthing love. Our only choice is to pay attention in the midst of the noise. When we do pay attention, we put Christ back into Christmas no matter what day the calendar says it is.

Put Christ back into Christmas? Sure, why not? He may smile at our attempts, but what he really wants is to find room in whatever day it is that love needs to be born.

The Christmas List

by Lucia Herndon

NOW THAT THE HOLIDAYS ARE UPON US, PARENTS across the land are either wringing their hands or holding aching heads in their hands as they contemplate this question: What do we get the kids this year?

If your household is like mine, written lists already have been submitted. My son's list usually has the item, its cost, and where it can be purchased. His list is long and expensive. My daughter is twenty, and her list is usually quite short, but just as expensive. Quality over quantity, she tells me.

This is the time of year that my son will ask me: "Are you sure we're not Jewish?" His Jewish friends will be collecting Hanukkah gifts for eight days, a better deal than one day of Christmas, to his thinking.

It seems the world has done a good job of telling children—and adults, too—what the end-of-the-year holidays are all about. Instead of enjoying the miracle of one day's oil lasting for a week, we spend dizzying hours in the mall. Instead of marveling at the birth of a baby who would change the world, we drive ourselves crazy with buying, eating, drinking.

This year we should recognize the message that our children are hearing all around them: that this time of year is one of unbridled gluttony and commercialism.

We should take ourselves firmly in hand and remind ourselves what these holidays mean. Then we can very clearly give our children the gifts they probably don't know they want but truly need. Taking note of an item published in the *Anglican Digest*, here's my list:

OUR ATTENTION. In our hectic world, time seems more precious than money. While we're willing to spend small fortunes on our children, we emulate Scrooge when it comes to sharing our time with them. Take time to pay attention to your children. Yes, sacrifice something and spend time with them. If you have more than one child, spend time with each child individually.

UNEXPECTED PRAISE. I remember a time when I would spout a litany of tasks I wanted the children to do. My son would look at me and snap, "Yes, Sergeant!" He made me realize that not only was I ordering him about, but I wasn't even stopping long enough to say "good job" when he finished. Surprise your child by saying "good job" when he least expects it. I guarantee you'll first be greeted by puzzlement and after the second or third time, a big grin.

AN IMPROMPTU KISS. Little kids glow with kisses. Bigger kids often keep the glow to themselves, but they like kisses just as much as toddlers. Try grabbing that taller-than-you teenager by the ears and planting a big kiss on his forehead. This is okay for dads to do, too. In fact, dads should definitely do this. Just remember not to do it in front of your child's friends.

A WORK ETHIC. Instilling in your child a willingness to work should begin early in her life. Children should grow up seeing their parents engaged in work around the house and outside the house. They should realize that work has a place in their lives, too, and that there is satisfaction to be gained in doing good work.

A STRAIGHT ANSWER. Sometimes simple things are the hardest to give. But what children need to hear is simple truth simply stated. No hemming or hawing. Just a straight answer is all that's necessary.

A SENSE OF HUMOR. Help your child see the humor in situations and, more important, in themselves. Teach them not to take themselves too seriously and to be able to laugh at their own shortcomings.

A SENSE OF WONDER. It's good to know, humbling to know, that there are things bigger than yourself. My children still delight in the power of a summer rainstorm. The crashing of thunder, the flashing of lightning still thrills them.

THE MEMORY OF A GOOD HOME. And I'm not talking about the house. Children should leave home with the aura of love and respect surrounding them. It will help them create their own good homes and is a living tribute to parents' teaching.

THE KNOWLEDGE OF BEING LOVED BEYOND DEMAND OR BLAME. Children should know they are loved not because society demands that parents love children or because we fear reprisals if we don't. Children should realize that love cannot be tallied by how obedient they are or how good their school grades are. There is no charge for parental love, and there is no way for children to repay parents for it.

Well, those are my Christmas gift list suggestions. Feel free to use them.

Lucia Herndon is a family columnist for The Philadelphia Inquirer. *Reprinted by permission from* The Philadelphia Inquirer.

CHRISTMAS
DRAMA

Emmanuel

A Christmas Musical for Young Children

by Rev. J. Lynn James

Setting the Stage

This musical is written so that all children who want a speaking part may have one. Lines may be spoken by one child or by a group, and may also be combined. Piano, organ, or guitar accompaniment is appropriate for the songs; they may also be sung a cappella. You will need to print the congregation's words in the bulletin or have them printed on "cue cards."

Props and scenery needed are: a manger (an orange crate filled with straw will do), a baby doll and a blanket for baby Jesus, gifts for the Wise Ones (fancy boxes or jars), and flashlights or electric candles for the Stars. *Emmanuel* is designed for a sanctuary, but any room will do. To get the full effect of the flashlights or electric candles, try to choose a room that can be darkened.

Adapt the following character guidelines to your own situation.

NARRATOR(S) should be older children or adults. Position them behind a pulpit or give them a microphone.

MARY and **JOSEPH** are fairly simple parts, so you may wish to choose younger children for these roles. Mary may wear a plain, adult-size T-shirt and a towel for a veil. Joseph may wear a shepherd-type outfit (see below).

ANIMALS include cows, donkeys and sheep. Choose your youngest children for these three groups. Masks may be made by the children in their Sunday school classes. Cut the center out of a paper plate and attach a craft stick for a handle; add cotton balls for sheep, construction-paper donkey ears or cow horns. Children may hold their masks up in front of their faces. You'll need another group of sheep to be with the shepherds.

SHEPHERDS (include both boys and girls) may wear the standard bathrobe and head kerchief held with a rope or stretchy headband.

ANGELS may make their own halos out of gold or silver tinsel garland. Each angel should wear white: an adult-size white T-shirt, a white sweatsuit, a white dress, and so on.

STARS should wear dark colors. Choose your oldest children for these parts, since they will need to operate flashlights or electric candles on cue.

WISE ONES may wear fancy bathrobes and construction-paper crowns. You may certainly use more than three children, and be sure to include some girls!

NARRATOR:	In those days a decree went out from Emperor Augustus that all the world should be registered. All went to their own towns to be registered. Joseph also went from the town of Nazareth in Galilee to Judea, to the city of David called Bethlehem, because he was descended from the house and family of David. He went to be registered with Mary, to whom he was engaged and who was expecting a child. While they were there, the time came for her to deliver her child.
MARY:	Joseph, we have traveled so far and we are both tired. The baby will be here soon. We must find a place to stop for the night.
JOSEPH:	Let's knock on the doors along this street. Surely somebody will let us in.
MARY AND JOSEPH:	(*walking up the aisle from the back of the sanctuary, knocking on pews*) Do you have a place for us?
CONGREGATION:	(*after each knock*) We're sorry, but our lives are too full. There is no room for you.

(*Mary and Joseph reach the stable in the front of the sanctuary. Animals all make their animal sounds.*)

COWS:	Our straw is soft and our stable is warm.
DONKEYS:	We will keep you safe from harm.
SHEEP:	We love everyone, it's true!
ALL:	And so of course we welcome you!
NARRATOR:	And she gave birth to her firstborn son and wrapped him in bands of cloth, and laid him in a manger, because there was no place for them in the inn.

(*Mary wraps Jesus in a blanket, kisses his forehead and lays him in the manger.*)

ANIMALS:	*Sing "Away in a Manger" (with sign language if possible).*
NARRATOR:	And Mary celebrated the birth of her child.
MARY:	(*sings a lullaby while rocking baby Jesus, to the tune of "Rock-a-bye-baby"*): Rock-a-bye Jesus, my precious boy, Being your mother fills me with joy. When the winds blow and trouble is near, Mama will hold you, never you fear.

(*Shepherds and their sheep enter and take places on steps or risers.*)

NARRATOR:	In that region there were shepherds living in the fields, keeping watch over their flock by night.
SHEPHERD:	Look! What's that up in the sky?
SHEPHERD:	It looks like an angel, way up high!
SHEPHERD:	It's coming closer! We'd better hide!

SHEPHERD:	Or run for the hills—I'm terrified!
NARRATOR:	The shepherds were filled with fear, but the angel said to them:
CONGREGATION:	Do not be afraid!
ANGEL:	For see—I am bringing you good news of great joy for all the people!
ANGEL:	To you is born this day in the city of David a Savior, who is the Messiah, the Lord!
ANGEL:	This will be a sign for you:
ANGEL:	You will find a child wrapped in bands of cloth and lying in a manger.
CONGREGATION:	Go take this message, tell it far and near, Emmanuel, Emmanuel, God is with us here!
NARRATOR:	And suddenly there was with the angel a multitude of the heavenly host, praising God and saying:
CONGREGATION:	Glory to God in the highest heaven, and on earth peace among those whom he favors!
CONGREGATION AND ANGELS:	(*sing 3 times to the tune of "Row, Row, Row Your Boat"*) Go, go, go to see who is born this night. A gift from God, this holy child Who comes to bring us light!
SHEPHERDS:	Let's all go to Bethlehem!

(*Shepherds and their sheep walk to the stable and sit beside the manger.*)

NARRATOR:	So they went with haste and found Mary and Joseph, and the child lying in the manger. When they saw this, they made known what had been told them about this child; and all who heard it were amazed at what the shepherds told them.
ALL:	(*Sing "Amen" chorus, then shepherds and their sheep sing first verse while everyone else sings chorus*): Amen, amen, Amen, amen, amen! See the little baby, Lying in a manger, On Christmas morning Amen, amen!
NARRATOR:	The shepherds returned, glorifying and praising God for all they had heard and seen, as it had been told them.
SHEPHERDS AND SHEEP:	Let's give thanks to God above! We've found Jesus and we'll share his love!

(Shepherds and their sheep exit.)

NARRATOR: All this took place to fulfill what had been spoken by the Lord through the prophet:

CONGREGATION: Look, the virgin shall conceive and bear a son, and they shall name him Emmanuel, which means "God is with us"!

ALL CHILDREN: *(sing to the tune of "The Muffin Man"):*
Emmanuel means God with us, God with us, God with us,
Emmanuel means God with us—we'll never be alone!

So if you feel alone and scared, alone and scared, alone and scared,
So if you feel alone and scared, remember Emmanuel!

(Stars take their places in various spots in the sanctuary and turn on their lights. Wise men enter from the back and walk halfway up the aisle, then stop.)

NARRATOR: In the time of King Herod, after Jesus was born in Bethlehem of Judea, wise ones from the East came to Jerusalem, asking:

WISE ONE: Where is the baby king?

WISE ONE: We have seen his star in the east.

WISE ONE: We have come to worship him.

NARRATOR: Then Herod secretly called for the wise ones and learned from them the exact time when the star had appeared. Then he sent them to Bethlehem saying, "Go and search diligently for the child; and when you have found him, bring me word so that I may go also and pay him homage." When they had heard the king, they set out; and there, ahead of them, went the star that they had seen at its rising, until it stopped over the place where the child was. When they saw that the star had stopped, they were overwhelmed with joy.

WISE ONES: *(continue walking up the aisle and sing to the tune of "Twinkle, Twinkle, Little Star"):*
Twinkle, twinkle, little star, how we wonder what you are,
Up above the world so high, like a diamond in the sky;
Twinkle, twinkle through the night, lead us with your special light.

Twinkle, twinkle, Christmas star, now we know just what you are.
Over hills and valleys we ride; Christmas star, please be our guide.
Take us to the newborn king; we have special gifts to bring!

(During the song, stars move to the front of the sanctuary and put their lights together. Wise ones go to the manger and kneel.)

NARRATOR: On entering the house, they saw the child with Mary his mother; and they knelt down and paid him homage. Then, opening their treasure chests, they offered him gifts of gold, frankincense, and myrrh.

WISE ONES: *(laying their gifts near the manger):*

We've brought treasures, one, two, three
And we give them gratefully.
But these gifts are just a start—
Best of all we give our hearts!

CHILDREN AND
CONGREGATION: *Sing "Silent Night"*

STAR: God's love shines above this stall.

STAR: God's love shines inside us all.

STAR: We'll shine our lights for everyone,

STAR: So they can see what God has done!

STAR: Because we have great news to tell—

ALL STARS: God's with us—Emmanuel!
(Sing chorus of "This Little Light of Mine"):
This little light of mine, I'm gonna let it shine,
This little light of mine, I'm gonna let it shine,
This little light of mine, I'm gonna let it shine,
Let it shine, let it shine, let it shine!

(Children and congregation join in for verses):

People who walked in darkness have seen a mighty light,
People who walked in darkness have seen a mighty light,
People who walked in darkness have seen a mighty light,
Seen it shine, seen it shine, seen it shine.

(chorus)

God's love's inside me and you, come on and let it shine!
God's love's inside me and you, come on and let it shine!
God's love's inside me and you, come on and let it shine!
Let it shine, let it shine, let it shine!

(chorus)

The Angel Said, Stop!

A Drama by Susan Kathleen Casey

Characters

DAD

MOM

ALLISON (17 years old)

SHAUN (12 years old—may be boy or girl)

CHRIS (8 years old—may be boy or girl)

Setting

The living room, Christmas Eve. Chaos reigns. On a small table is a phone with the receiver off the hook. Throughout CHRIS remains stationary, sitting on a stool or tall chair, while the action swirls around him/her.

CHRIS: I can't believe it's only six o'clock! Christmas Eve must be the longest day of the year. *(fidgets a little, then sighs)*

(MOM enters carrying wrapping paper.)

MOM: Where did I put Aunt Kate's package? *(looks frantically around the room)* I had the package in my hands. And the phone rang. Aunt Ann wanted my recipe for spinach dip, so I went to the kitchen. Then Allison wanted my sewing scissors . . . and the timer went on my cookies . . . and—oh, dear, the phone, Aunt Ann! *(heads toward phone)*

CHRIS: Mom, I think I smell something burning.

MOM: My cookies! *(runs off)*

(ALLISON enters carrying a costume for a Christmas pageant.)

ALLISON: Hey, Chris, have you seen Mom? I need scissors . . .

CHRIS: She's in the kitchen.

(ALLISON dashes off without hearing. SHAUN enters.)

SHAUN: Mr. Cameron was supposed to call ages ago. We're going caroling with the youth group after the service tonight. I hope Tom's mom can drive, or we'll have to see if Jen's older brother can borrow his grandma's car, and—(*sees the phone off the hook*). Hey! Who left the phone off the hook? (*picks it up*) Hello? Aunt Ann! What spinach recipe? Hey, Chris, where's—

CHRIS: Kitchen.

(*SHAUN dashes off. ALLISON races back in, still carrying the costume. DAD enters from the opposite direction, intently reading a sheet of directions and muttering under his breath. They collide.*)

DAD: Whoa! Has anyone seen my Phillips head screwdriver? Where's your—?

CHRIS AND ALLISON: Kitchen!

(*DAD exits to kitchen.*)

ALLISON: You haven't seen my wings, have you, Chris?

CHRIS: Nope.

ALLISON: How am I supposed to be the Angel Gabriel without wings?

CHRIS: You could flap your arms. (*demonstrates*)

ALLISON: Oh, great! Then I'd look like the Chicken Gabriel.

CHRIS: How much longer till we go to church?

ALLISON: Not long enough! (*looking around frantically*)

CHRIS: It seems like forever. And even longer till we go to bed. And really, *really* long until tomorrow.

ALLISON: (*reminiscing*): I remember when I felt that way. (*sighs*) It's sure different now. (*Looks under a sofa pillow for wings, spots a Bible.*) Hey, Chris, why don't you read about the Christmas story? Maybe it'll make the time go faster.

(*ALLISON hands the Bible to CHRIS, then rushes out. MOM rushes in holding wrapping paper and scissors.*)

MOM: I have those scissors. Where's Allison?

CHRIS: Looking for wings.

MOM: What?

CHRIS: Wings. Allison can't find Gabriel's wings.

MOM: (*muttering*) Wings . . . wings . . . wings?

CHRIS: Mom, where's the Christmas story?

MOM:	Wings. *(looks at CHRIS)* What, dear?
CHRIS:	*(holding up Bible)* The Christmas story. Where is it?
MOM:	Oh. It's in Luke. The second chapter of Luke.
CHRIS:	*(flips through the Bible)* Allison said time might go faster if I read the Christmas story.
MOM:	*(only half listening)* That's wonderful . . . hmm . . . wings . . .

(MOM rushes out still holding scissors and wrapping paper. SHAUN enters with a recipe card and heads toward the phone. DAD enters.)

DAD:	It's not in the kitchen.
SHAUN:	What's not?
DAD:	The Phillips head screwdriver.
SHAUN:	I think I saw it on the dining room table. Under the garland boxes, next to the Christmas cards that Mom's still working on. *(sees DAD'S puzzled face)* I'll go look.

(SHAUN exits, still holding the recipe card.)

CHRIS:	What's a census?
DAD:	Huh?
CHRIS:	A census.
DAD:	It's when the government counts everybody. Why?
CHRIS:	I'm reading the Christmas story.
DAD:	That's nice.

(SHAUN enters with screwdriver and recipe card.)

SHAUN:	Found it. *(hands screwdriver to DAD)*
DAD:	Great! Now if I can only figure out how Piece "Q" is supposed to connect to Pieces "E" and "J."
CHRIS:	What are you making, Dad?
DAD:	Oh . . . um . . . well . . . nothing . . . er . . .

(DAD exits quickly.)

CHRIS:	He's probably putting together my WildWheels Super Flyer.
SHAUN:	*(sees phone)* Aunt Ann!!

(*SHAUN runs to the phone. ALLISON and MOM enter, still carrying costume and wrapping paper.*)

MOM: Where were you when you last had your wings?

SHAUN: Those strange-looking gold things with the sequins and wire?

ALLISON: (*excitedly*) Have you seen them?

SHAUN: I think I saw them in the basement.

(*SHAUN puts down the phone and exits to the basement, still carrying the recipe card.*)

CHRIS: What's a manger?

MOM: What? (*looks blankly at Chris*) Oh, a manger. Something that holds food for animals to eat.

CHRIS: Like Spike's dish?

ALLISON: Not quite. It's bigger.

MOM: Spike! Has anyone let the dog out yet? He hasn't been out since— (*thinks, then panics*) Spike! Come here, Spike!

(*MOM runs off. DAD enters holding the screwdriver and an unidentifiable piece of plastic. SHAUN enters with him, still holding the recipe card.*)

DAD: I still don't have any idea what this is.

SHAUN: Beats me. (*to ALLISON*) No wings.

ALLISON: Aaack!

(*ALLISON begins frantically hunting for wings, knocking over the phone.*)

SHAUN: Aunt Ann!! (*runs to the phone and picks it up*) Aunt Ann? Are you still there? Things are a little crazy here . . .

(*MOM rushes in.*)

MOM: A mop. I need newspaper and a mop . . . or an old towel, or . . .

DAD: Maybe it's part of Gear Mechanism "G."

SHAUN: (*into phone*) Two packages of frozen spinach . . .

ALLISON: Wings! Where did I put those wings??

CHRIS: (*one hand over his/her ear*) "And an angel of the Lord appeared to them . . ."

DAD: The brake system?

MOM: Newspaper!

SHAUN: *(into phone)* No, not sour cream . . .

ALLISON: *(desperately)* Wings!

CHRIS: *(reading louder)* "But the angel said to them . . ."

DAD: Handlebars!

SHAUN: A pinch of garlic . . .

ALLISON: We have to leave in five minutes! Where are my wings??

CHRIS: "The angel said . . ." *(louder)* "The angel said . . . STOP!"

(ALL stop suddenly and stare at CHRIS.)

ALLISON: No, that's my line. "The angel said—"

DAD: Maybe Chris is right.

MOM: What?

DAD: Think a minute. The shepherds stopped. They stopped to listen. And then they stopped what they were doing, to go—to go to Bethlehem.

SHAUN: Yeah, I guess they did.

DAD: They had to stop, because when Jesus came, everything changed. God came to be with us, to live with us. That's why we celebrate Christmas.

MOM: By running around . . .

ALLISON: Like we always do . . .

SHAUN: Only worse.

(DAD takes the Bible from CHRIS.)

DAD: *(reading)* "In those days Caesar Augustus issued a decree that a census should be taken of the entire Roman world. (This was the first census that took place while Quirinius was governor of Syria.) And everyone went to his own town to register."

(DAD hands the Bible to MOM.)

MOM: "So Joseph also went up from the town of Nazareth in Galilee to Judea, to Bethlehem the town of David, because he belonged to the house and line of David. He went there to register with Mary, who was pledged to be married to him and was expecting a child. While they were there, the time came for the baby to be born, and she gave birth to her firstborn, a son. She wrapped him in strips of cloth and placed him in a manger, because there was no room for them in the inn."

(*MOM hands Bible to SHAUN.*)

SHAUN: "And there were shepherds living out in the fields nearby, keeping watch over their flocks at night. An angel of the Lord appeared to them, and the glory of the Lord shone around them, and they were terrified. But the angel said to them, . . ."

ALLISON: (*smiling and reciting from memory*) "'Do not be afraid. I bring you good news of great joy that will be for all the people. Today in the town of David a Savior has been born to you; he is Christ the Lord. This will be a sign to you: You will find a baby wrapped in strips of cloth and lying in a manger.'"

DAD: I think they'll finish the story at church tonight. Let's go.

(*SHAUN puts down the Bible. DAD lifts CHRIS off the stool. All but SHAUN quietly leave for church. SHAUN picks up the phone.*)

SHAUN: Aunt Ann? We're leaving for church now. We decided to stop and celebrate Christmas.

(*SHAUN gently hangs up the phone and then leaves.*)

CHRISTMAS
IN VERSE

An Advent Prayer

by Israel Galindo

OUR GOD,
You whose promises are sure and secure,

We enter into this season of disciplined anticipation
    with the disadvantage of the knowledge of the outcome—
        we know how this familiar story will turn out.

OUR GOD OF ADVENT,
we confess that mysteries seem a thing of the past in our lives;
even children who once made wish lists in hope,
    today leave marked-up colored catalogues
    as non-subtle hints of implied good behavior.
With no mysteries under the tree,
    they too, have lost the mystery of anticipation,
        we fear.

In our hurried lives, we need the gift of anticipation,
    for we have lost the ability to wait,
    to cherish the moment,
    to embrace uncertainty
        and so, often, to live by faith.

WE CRAVE CERTITUDE, OUR GOD,

    in uncertain times,

in the fear of threats to body and spirit,

we crave answers and solutions;

But you give us mysteries, angel visitations,

    and ask us to wait for "that day."

And so we ask for the gift of anticipation,

that we may believe and live in the

    humble spirit of a young girl

    given a gift, whispered a mystery,

    and told to wait for God to act, in that day.

IN THIS ADVENT SEASON, OUR GOD,

    give us this gift, that we too may see your

    mysteries unfold in our lives.

For we pray in the name of the Christ Child

    who is our Savior,

      Jesus Christ.

      Amen.

Boundary to Benedictus

A Meditation on Zechariah

by Kenneth L. Sehested

ZECHARIAH—
hillbilly priest of the
Abijarian house of Aaron,
himself the brother and mouthpiece
for "slow-tongued" Moses—
What lesion confounds your speech?

With Elizabeth—
cousin of Mary, spiritual heir of
Sarah, Rebekah, Rachel and Hannah—
barren and bereft, seedless and sorrowful.
A priest of impotent prayer,
A union with no yield but malignant shame.
What boundary of belief constricts your credulity?

Afflicted with aphasia by Gabriel's reproach
'mid the cloud of incense.
The Holy of Holies,
designed to regulate the presence of YHWH
(unspoken name of the Holy One of Israel)
now overwhelmed with dumbfounding Presence.

From your seed (and Elizabeth's
fallow soil) shall spring
   John—Naziritic preamble to Mary's manifesto
   John—whose conception prompts
Judean astonishment: "What then will this child be?"

SPEECHLESS ZECHARIAH,
befuddled cleric,
schooled in the theory of divine history
but unacquainted with its Advent.
For us, too, encountering the One
who promises the impossible
is a confusing, confounding prospect.
New life issues with a scream,
but is forged in the ordeal
of muted mouth.

Yet after a sojourn in the
wilderness of that bewilderment
even the silence gives way
to benedictus, to blessing.
The promise of perplexity
(for those willing to risk)
is praise and wombs leaping in joy.

Only by this unraveling
is the darkness dispelled,
is life re-raveled, is the boundary to
benedictus transgressed and the
tongue loosened for laudation.

JOHN, TOO—
whose very name transcends
ancestral boundary—
will reside in his own wilderness
until the time of harvest vocation:
    to turn
the hearts of parents to their children
    to give
light to those who sit in the shadow of death
    to guide
our feet to the way of peace.

A Christmas Desiderata

by Margaret Anne Huffman

Mend a fight Get in touch with distant friends Thank clerks who need a kind word Encourage kids Keep promises Find time Sit in the dark Listen Smell Laugh aloud Think first of someone else Enjoy the beauty of the winter earth Welcome a stranger Apologize if you're wrong Give up a grudge Forgive an enemy Make soup and share it Look without suspicion at strangers Trim your calendar where you can Give someone a hug Make angels in the snow Take a nap Hold a hand Call a friend Sing a carol Take a hot bath Look at the stars Go sledding Whistle Do a favor for someone Say "thank you" Read the Christmas story aloud Skip Play a game Be thankful for all the gifts that you have already

CHRISTMAS
CRAFTS
For Church and Home

Advent Wreaths

ADVENT WREATHS CAN BE MADE FROM JUST ABOUT anything circular and decorated with anything green—or any other color, for that matter. Try one of these Advent wreath ideas if you're looking for something just a little bit different this year.

Pine Cone Wreath

MATERIALS:

- An inexpensive, purchased metal Advent wreath ring
- Lots of pine cones, of all shapes and sizes
- Assorted nuts and dried pods
- Hot glue gun, if available; otherwise good white craft glue

1. Sort out 12–16 long, narrow pine cones and soak them in water for about an hour until they close up. Then insert the cones between the upper and lower wires on the wreath ring, between the candle holders. Set the ring aside for at least two days to allow the pine cones to dry.

2. When the cones are dry and have opened, they should stay inside the ring by themselves; if any are loose, apply some glue. Then begin gluing on other pine cones, nuts, and pods in whatever arrangement pleases you. You can make pine cone "flowers" by cutting rounder cones in half.

3. After the wreath is assembled and glue is dry, spray it with clear shellac.

For-Kids-Only Advent Wreath

MATERIALS:

- Cardboard egg carton
- Small (9-inch) pizza round
- Poster paint
- Small taper-type Advent candles

1. Cut the center out of the pizza round, leaving a 3-inch-wide ring. Cut apart the egg carton into six double cups.

2. Arrange the cups upside-down around the cardboard ring; make sure they are all touching each other in a circle. Glue the cups to the ring in this arrangement.

3. Paint your wreath in whatever way you like. You may want to add some red berries or a bow, snowflakes, birds—anything!

4. Using a pencil or pen, poke a hole in the top of four of the egg cups. Make sure the holes are not too big! Insert an Advent candle in each of the holes. Use your Advent wreath in your family Advent services.

The No-Wreath Wreath

Purchase five column-type and/or round candles of varying heights and widths: three purple, one pink, and one white. Arrange them in a cluster and surround them with something beautiful: greenery, ribbon, small Christmas ornaments, straw, dried grapevine, shiny tinsel.

Candles

CHRISTMAS WOULD HARDLY BE CHRISTMAS WITHOUT candlelight. No other kind of light communicates so well that Jesus is the Light of the world. This year try making your own candles. Anyone can do it, but you'll have more success if you use the special candle wax, paraffin, dyes, and wicks easily obtainable from a craft store. You may dip your own Advent candles, or try some of these more unusual candle-making ideas.

Fire-and-Ice Candles

MATERIALS:

- Quart-size milk carton; cut the top off
- Candle wax or paraffin
- Taper-type candle for center core
- Ice cubes

1. Melt wax over low heat in a double boiler. Pour about ½ inch of wax into the bottom of the milk carton. Put the taper candle into the center of the milk carton and hold it in place until the wax dries.

2. Carefully fill up the milk carton with ice cubes. The more varied in shape your ice cubes, the more interesting your candle will be. Then gradually pour in the melted wax. The wax will harden as the ice cubes melt, leaving holes (the Swiss cheese principle).

3. Pour off the melted ice and allow the candle to harden completely. Then peel off the milk carton. If you used a colored core candle, it will glow brightly through the holes.

Dipped and Braided Candles

MATERIALS:

- Large cake pan or jellyroll pan
- Colored wax or paraffin
- Wicking
- Wax paper

Heat wax in the cake pan and keep it at about 150 degrees. Cut three strands of wick about 12 inches long. Pull a strand through the wax; wait a few seconds, then pull it through again. Repeat at least two more times. Lay the strand on the wax paper. Then repeat the procedure with the other two strands. Working very quickly, braid the three strands together while the wax is still pliable. Pinch the ends together. These candles will burn with a much larger flame because of the three wicks. (If you are skilled at macramé, the knotting possibilities are endless!)

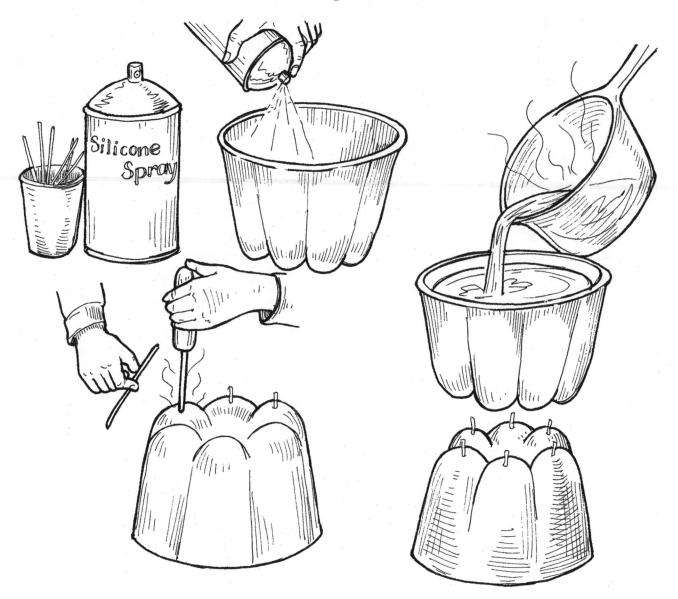

Gelatin Mold Multi-Wick Candle

MATERIALS:

- Gelatin mold with interesting shape
- Silicone spray
- Candle wax or paraffin
- Wire wicks
- Ice pick or knitting needle

1. Spray a gelatin mold with silicone spray and let it dry. Melt your wax in a double boiler over low heat. Gradually pour it into the mold. If you are using different colors of wax, pour it into the mold in layers, letting each layer harden before adding the next. Allow the candle to harden completely.

2. Turn the mold upside down and remove the candle. Using a heated ice pick or knitting needle, poke a hole in several of the "bumps." Insert a wire wick into each hole.

Origami and Paper Crafts

THE JAPANESE ART OF PAPER FOLDING IS A GREAT activity for long winter afternoons. Both children and adults will enjoy making these simple yet beautiful paper decorations.

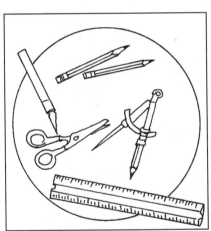

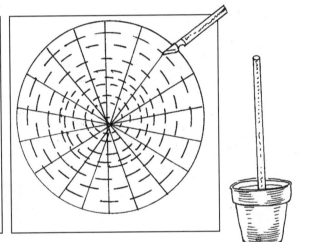

Lacy Christmas Tree

MATERIALS:

- Large circle (about 20 inches in diameter) of sturdy, lightweight colored paper (not construction paper—it will tear)
- Compass or ruler
- Red and blue colored pencils
- Scissors or X-acto knife

1. Lay the paper circle on top of a sheet of cardboard. Using the compass or measuring with a ruler, draw concentric circles at $1/2$-inch intervals from the outside of the circle to the center. Use two different colored pencils to draw the circles, alternating them (i.e., blue, red, blue, red). Then use the ruler to draw lines dividing the circle into twentieths.

2. Make a slit with scissors or X-acto knife on **only** the blue circular lines at each point where a concentric circle is crossed by a diametric line. Begin at the center. The further out you go, the longer your slits should be. Now go back to the center and make slits on the red circular lines, but this time **between** the diametric lines.

3. Carefully lift the paper circle from beneath and tug gently all the way around to separate the slits. You may suspend your lacy tree by a string attached to the center, or drape it over a "trunk." Add a pleated star to the top.

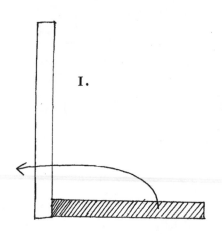

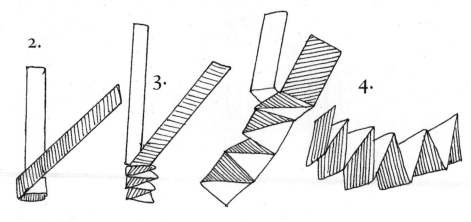

Stairstep Garlands

MATERIALS:

- Strips of origami or construction paper, ½-inch wide, in holiday colors
- Glue

1. Glue two different colored strips together at a right angle (L-shape).

2. Fold one strip over the other, back and forth, until your strips become a stack. If you want a longer garland, glue on another two strips and continue folding.

3. When your garland is long enough, glue the ends of the two strips together.

4. When the garland is completely dry, pull slightly on the ends to expose the folded colors.

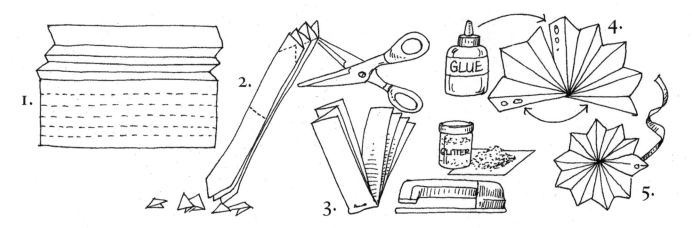

Pleated Star

MATERIALS:

- Rectangular sheet of origami or construction paper
- Scissors
- Glue
- Glitter
- Ribbon

1. Starting at the short side, pleat (accordion-fold) a sheet of construction paper. While folded, cut off each end in a scalloped edge.

2. Pinch the pleated paper in the center (you may wish to staple it) and then bring the two corners of one long side together. Glue them together. Do the same with the corners on the other side.

3. Decorate your star with glue and glitter. Attach a ribbon for a hanger.

CHRISTMAS
CELEBRATIONS

Hanging of the Greens

A Service of Worship for the First Sunday in Advent

by Gary L. McCann

What have Christmas trees, wreaths, sprigs of holly, mistletoe, and poinsettias to do with the Christian celebration of Christmas? Everything! All too often the Christian church has separated the religious and secular elements of this festive holiday at the expense of enjoying the season's rich heritage.

A "hanging of the greens" service can help Christians rediscover the valuable meaning of these Christmas symbols. More than just a social get-together to "decorate" the sanctuary, this service of worship involves the whole congregation and includes both young and old, celebrating the mystery of the season and the incarnation of our Lord. Many variations exist. Each church may tailor the script to its own needs and resources.

ORGAN PRELUDE

PROCESSIONAL

HYMN: "O Come, All Ye Faithful" *(Madrigal singers or choir process with clergy)*

CALL TO WORSHIP

LEADER: The people who walked in darkness have seen a great light.

PEOPLE: For a child has been born for us; a Son given to us.

LEADER: He is named Wonderful Counselor, Mighty God, Everlasting Father, Prince of Peace.

PEOPLE: His authority shall grow continually and there shall be endless peace.

ALL: O Holy Child of Bethlehem!   We hear the Christmas angels
Descend to us, we pray;   The great glad tidings tell;
Cast out our sin and enter in;   O come to us, abide with us,
Be born in us today.   Our Lord Emmanuel! Amen.

PRAYER

SCRIPTURE
LESSON: Isaiah 40:1–5 *(Read in unison with the congregation; use pew Bibles or print text)*

VOCAL
SOLO: "Comfort Ye" from Messiah

PROCLAMATION OF GOD'S WORD
(Minister prepares a brief sermon that introduces the Advent theme and prepares the congregation for the presentation of the greens.)

HANGING OF THE GREENS
LEADER: We're bringing in the Christmas greens, the symbols, the traditions that make Christmas so unique.

PEOPLE: We're bringing holly, mistletoe, evergreens to decorate this sanctuary to remind us of Christmas love and cheer.

LEADER: Everywhere in homes and churches we hang the Christmas greens.

PEOPLE: And now in our joy and merriment, we call to mind the meaning of each of the symbols.

ALL: For these are symbols to remind us of the gift God gave us in Jesus.

HYMN: "O Come, O Come Emmanuel"

The Greens

Select two or three readers for the following paragraphs. As these paragraphs are read, involve a variety of people in carrying the particular items mentioned to the front of the church. Have a place for every item in the chancel. After placing the object in its place, the person returns to his or her seat. A Saturday morning rehearsal is helpful.

Bring in the greens, the pine, the fir, the cedar—all are part of Christmas joy. They remind us, when all is bare and barren, of the promised reawakening of the earth in spring. Early Christians decorated the sanctuary with the evergreen as a promise of new life and a sign of hope that in Christ all live forever. Early belief was that evergreens symbolized the blessing of everlasting life. In Isaiah 60:13 we find these words: "The glory of Lebanon shall come to you, the cypress, the plane and the pine, to beautify the place of my sanctuary."

HYMN: "Go Tell It on the Mountain"

The Holly

Gleaming brightly in the light of Christmas candles, the glistening leaves and shining berries of the holly remind us of the joy and happiness that comes to humankind in the birth of God's Son. In the midst of a bleak, dead winter the green leaves speak to us of life, and the red berries remind us of the blood our Lord shed so that we might have life.

MADRIGAL SINGERS
OR CHOIR: "The Holly and the Ivy"

The Mistletoe

The mistletoe has become for us the symbol of merriment, the sign of a kiss. But in ancient times two warriors meeting under the mistletoe threw down their weapons and embraced in brotherhood. Thus it became the custom of early Christians to place a spray of mistletoe upon the altar at Christmastime to remind the worshiper of the power and peace of Christ to heal the body and the soul.

HYMN: "Let There Be Peace on Earth"

The Christmas Tree

Best loved of all Christmas greens is the Christmas tree, bedecked with shining ornaments and sparkling lights. Upon its branches and beneath its boughs we place our gifts of love. The Chrismons,* Christ's Monograms, are placed on the tree to remind us of the life of our Lord born at this Christmastime. Each is a symbol of Jesus, and as we see these Chrismons each week during Advent, we are reminded of the coming of our Lord at his first advent and at his second.

The Magi brought their gifts, expensive gifts, to lay at the feet of the Christ Child. But gifts need not be expensive to be appreciated by God. They need only be from the heart, as was the gift given by the Good King Wenceslas. It is our Christmas trees in homes and churches that become the gathering places for these gifts.

MADRIGAL SINGERS
OR CHOIR: "Good King Wenceslas"

*Chrismons, or monograms of Christ, are symbols that honor the name of our Lord Jesus Christ. Symbols such as the cross and fish are made into Christmas tree ornaments of white, silver, and gold.

OFFERING

We offer our gifts because God first made a gift to us of Jesus. May you receive these gifts, O God, in the spirit with which they are given to you. Amen.

The Poinsettia

Jesus has been described as the Rose of Sharon, the Christmas rose. His life reminds us of the fragrance of flowers, the beauty of the petals, the freshness of the leaves. No sanctuary would be completely dressed without the beauty of these flowers.

The custom of decorating churches, homes and marketplaces with poinsettias had its origin in Mexico and Central America where the "fire flower" has been the source of many legends. One tells of a poor peasant girl who had no gift for the Christ Child to place at the altar on Christmas Eve. As she wept with sorrow an angel appeared to her and directed her to gather a bouquet of tall weeds that grew nearby and to present them as her gift. The girl obeyed, and as she laid them on the altar the weeds burst into a glorious red bloom. (*If your crèche is not already assembled, have people bring forward the figures during the next hymn.*)

MADRIGAL SINGERS
OR CHOIR: "Lo, How a Rose E'er Blooming"

The Christmas Crèche

Now with the beauty of the greens to remind us of the glory that came to earth at Christmas, let us hear again the story of the birth of Christ, the light of the world, as we focus on the scene described for us in Scripture and song.

HYMN: "O Little Town of Bethlehem" (verses 1 and 2)

SCRIPTURE: The Birth of Christ (*Read Luke 2:1–7 in unison from pew Bibles or printed text.*)

HYMN: "Away in a Manger" (verse 1)

SCRIPTURE: The Shepherds (*Read Luke 2:8-16 in unison.*)

The Christ Child

There is one person yet missing from the scene, the most important person in the whole drama. This is the baby, this Jesus, for whom the whole world sings and for whom we have decorated this church today. But we will not put his symbol in the crèche today, for this is only Advent, a time to prepare for his coming. Let us wait, let us anticipate, let us prepare, and then on Christmas Eve we shall place the Child in the manger to remind us of his birth.

HYMN: "Come, Thou Long-Expected Jesus" (verse 1)

THE ADVENT WREATH *(Light the first candle during the hymn, symbolizing expectation and hope.)*

SILENT MEDITATION

BENEDICTION

POSTLUDE

Does Santa Belong in Church?

Rediscovering the Feast Day of Nicholas of Myra

by Robert S. Reid

H OW SHOULD CHURCHES RESPOND TO THE WHOLE Santa Claus tradition? One member of my parish recently remarked, "Oh, he was banned around here a long time ago." Yet, on the same day I read in the newsletter of one of our sister congregations an announcement of the annual Christmas party for children with a visit from "you know who." Is it really an all-or-nothing tradition?

When my family decided that neither giving in nor withdrawing was the best response, we did some spadework on good old Saint Nick. The result was our discovery of the Feast Day of Saint Nicholas. The original story of Bishop Nicholas of Myra and his gracious acts of mercy lies at the heart of much of our Christmas tradition. Our family became convinced that sharing our "stocking gifts" on his real feast day was an effective way to positively defuse the "Christmas machine." We were able to establish the true story of Santa Claus and joyously allow our children to understand how one act of mercy has tumbled down through the centuries in a joyous tale of a cherry-cheeked old elf. The Feast Day of Nicholas of Myra is now a wonder-filled portion of our Advent celebration.

Part of our task in ministry is to find creative ways to help families in our churches recover the sense that it really can be a "blessed season." For many Christian teachers and parents, the question seems to be how best to respond to the ever-present Santa Claus. Jolly Old Saint Nicholas seems to possess an invincible

durability that can outlast even the toughest jeers of our jaded peers. Somehow this venerable old saint still manages to embody the mirth and good tidings of the Christmas season and to dominate what most of our school districts now must call the winter program.

Celebrate the Feast Day of Nicholas of Myra

As church teachers and leaders search for creative ways to add new vitality to their Advent celebration, the Feast Day of Nicholas of Myra can provide a unique opportunity. A congregation and its families may be able to reclaim the best part of Saint Nick's charm before he gets completely lost in the trail of his heavenly host of "eight tiny reindeer."

For centuries the Christian church has celebrated Saint Nicholas's day on December 6, a day that falls reasonably early in the traditional Advent celebration. Nestled far enough past Thanksgiving to allow stouthearted workers to marshal their forces, this date still permits parents and teachers to have a solid lead on the momentum that builds toward the fateful night of "dancing sugarplums." It may also allow many children, families, and teachers an opportunity to regain some of the joy of stocking gifts that are so often dwarfed by the brightly bundled boxes that engulf our trees.

But why should we reinstate the celebration of a feast day for Nicholas of Myra? To get beneath the layers of tradition of that "right jolly old elf," we need to rediscover the story of this patron saint of children, a story that has demonstrated an amazing resilience as it has come to us down through the centuries.

Bishop Nicholas of Myra

Surviving Byzantine carvings and paintings help us to uncover Nicholas's popular trail. His image was occasionally thin and forbidding, while at other times he was depicted as splendidly robed with a glorious bishop's miter and scepter. By the twelfth century his popularity was so great that he stood third in line following Jesus and Mary as the recipient of the hopes and prayers of the common people. The Protestant reformers vigorously tried to eliminate his "cult," for by that time the line between the worship of God and the veneration of the saints had virtually collapsed. But Nicholas of Myra had a tenacity that even Luther could not chase out of the German heritage.

The actual Nicholas appears to have been born in Patara, now part of modern-day Turkey, possibly in the year A.D. 280. He eventually became the bishop of the town of Myra, a coastal Mediterranean village. He appears to have been one of more than three hundred participating church leaders at the First Council of Nicea in A.D. 325. But tradition could not allow Nicholas merely to attend. As Arius (a cleric who was denounced as a heretic) spoke, Nicholas is said to have been so outraged by the heresy being presented that he walked up to the speaker and struck him across the face. This audacious action was supposedly vindicated by a private visitation of the risen Lord and his mother. It was the testimony of that vision that was said to have swayed the vote of the council against Arius.

Sainthood is built on authenticating miracles, and many stories flourished. Nicholas eventually became known as the saint who was always ready to help wherever need existed. Through several stories of miraculous deliverances, he became known throughout eastern Europe as the patron saint of sailors.

Yet, under all of the trappings of legends comes the simple tale of a pastor who once helped a poor man to marry off each of his three daughters. Each time the family thought all was lost because of not having a dowry for the bride-to-be, the pastor secretly passed a stocking filled with three hundred florins

through the window. Unmasked during his third mission of mercy, Saint Nicholas was respected in silence throughout his life. Then, as so often happens when good and honorable people are venerated after their death, this one disarming anecdote inspired many stories of miraculous occurrences. One such tale, which involved the resurrection of three children who had been gruesomely killed, established Nicholas as the patron saint of all children.

Saint Nicholas in the New World

Curiously enough it was his dual role as patron saint of sailors and children that eventually inspired some citizens of New York City to add some color to their own limited heritage in the New World. One of our country's first noted literary works is the fancifully concocted *Dietrich Knickerbocker's History of New York from the Beginning of the World to the End of the Dutch Dynasty* by Washington Irving. In a crucial portion in the history of the founding of New York, one of the characters describes a dream in which the bust of Saint Nicholas leaves its carved post on the bow of the ship to make generous provision in picking just the right site for the Dutch settlers in founding their town. Thus begins the tale of Saint Nicholas's relationship as the patron saint of New York. Yet this particular Saint Nicholas has none of the demeanor of the ancient bishop of Myra. Instead, he sounds suspiciously like a pipe-smoking, rosy-cheeked Dutchman.

A second New Yorker, Clement Clarke Moore, drew upon this image when he penned a delightful poem to be read to his daughters and a few guests on the evening of December 23, 1822. Moore was a leading Hebrew scholar and one of the founding faculty of the General Theological Seminary of New York. He enjoyed writing verse as a hobby. Clement Moore could hardly have guessed that he would be forever immortalized by creating a small flight of fancy that began, "'Twas the night before Christmas . . .''

Within a few decades the New York artist Thomas Nast completed the reformulation of Saint Nicholas by visually creating the character described in Moore's inimitable poem. Nast drew his now famous depiction of Saint Nicholas with thoughtful

re-creations of images of his boyhood in Bavaria with its observance of lighted festival trees to celebrate the Christmas season. Much of the raw material for the Santa Claus legend is quite Christian and European, but the final creation is a uniquely American product of the city of New York.

So Nicholas of Myra evolved into Santa Claus because times and needs change. Previous generations desired a patron saint of protection. Our age, on the other hand, seems to yearn for the spirit of altruism embodied in a kindly father figure who cares for children of all generations. He has become someone who graciously, generously, and secretly provides for us at the time we need him. Legends lent his name to a multitude of needs, but at its heart his story tells of how mercy overcomes circumstances.

Meanings for Today

For young minds Nicholas of Myra's story can effectively convey the message of Advent—God's mercy and provision unwrapped in the face of judgment. His traditional feast day is a day to fill stockings with mercy just as Nicholas had once provided another family with merciful provision. Even Clement Moore's Saint Nicholas silently filled the children's stockings with gifts.

The tradition of small gifts placed in hanging stockings seems to be passing away. Our Christmas present extravaganzas overshadow most of the "stocking stuffers." Yet, it is the stocking part of Christmas that is most traditionally associated with Saint Nicholas and his act of mercy toward others. With all its humility, the stocking could be recovered as part of the real meaning of Christmas gift giving in our Advent celebration.

Using the Message of Saint Nicholas

In the Church School

If handled with sensitivity and the proper preparation, the true story of Santa Claus can be told as an example of a person of Christ who acted in love to provide for others. The wise teacher would want to alert parents that talking about Santa would be part of the Sunday church school session on a certain date. When the material is presented as an attempt to reclaim our true heritage for the education and enjoyment of our children, we can begin to transcend the polarized reactions of "giving in" to Santa Claus or "saying nothing"—the two reactions that seem to characterize many of our churches and their Sunday schools.

By seeing an analogy between Saint Nicholas's secret gift to the poor and God being "secreted" into the world in the coming of Christ, older children can make the association between the observance of Saint Nicholas's act of mercy and love and that of God in Christ.

Children can be encouraged to think about ways that they might help others who have needs as a symbol of the mercy that God expressed in sending Jesus Christ into the world and as a symbol of the mercy that Nicholas of Myra expressed when he provided the money for the dowries of each of the three daughters. The class might collect food or presents to give to organizations that help others in the tradition of Nicholas of Myra.

Children could suggest several practical projects of giving in which they could act with the same love and mercy that Saint Nicholas demonstrated.

The class might be highly stimulated if three separate "stockings of mercy" were quite suddenly flung into the room during the practical project time. Rather than "goodies," the stockings might contain those things that could be merciful provisions for a needy person. The "stocking of mercy" cast into the room may prompt discussion about who might need the kind of mercy expressed by the contents of the stocking.

In the Worship Service or Advent Program

After some of the tradition is conveyed, members of the congregation could be encouraged to participate in a "stockings of mercy" or "stockings of sharing" campaign. The stockings would be given to needy people in the name of Nicholas of Myra, who served the Lord of Christmas.

The story of Saint Nicholas could be shared during the lighting of the second Advent candle.

In the Home

Families could be encouraged to observe the Feast Day of Nicholas of Myra as part of the home Advent celebration. Churches could provide materials to help parents effectively share his story and the relationship of this godly person to Santa Claus.

Simple stockings of mercy could be shared at this time of the Christmas season rather than on December 25. Small stocking stuffers could provide a wonderful opportunity to reclaim our own heritage.

Special reading of joyful stories about Saint Nicholas, both factual and fanciful, could enhance the learning experience and the family time during this festive day. Information can be found in such resources as Harold Myra's excellent retelling of the Saint Nicholas story in *Santa, Are You for Real?* (Nashville: Thomas Nelson Inc., 1977) and short readings such as Clement Clarke Moore's "'Twas the Night Before Christmas" or the widely anthologized editor's response in the September 21, 1897, edition of the *New York Sun* entitled "Yes, Virginia, There Is a Santa Claus."

Family members could give other family members mercy presents—that time, thing, or experience that would show mercy during the Christmas season.

The feast day could involve a "Myra dinner," an occasion when new friends could be invited to share in the gift of hospitality and friendship.

This year rather than merely decrying the commercialization of the season, take time early in Advent to form the kind of church and family traditions that will reclaim the joy of giving as part of Advent.

From Shopping Mall to Sanctuary

An Advent Values Experience for Youth or Adults

by Julia Bebeau

IT HAPPENS EVERY YEAR. AS DECEMBER NEARS, WE ALL know that we'll get caught by it in some way: the Christmas Crunch. Cards to write, gifts to buy and wrap and mail, goodies to bake, parties and church functions and school programs to attend—the list goes on and on, and with it comes a mounting anxiousness. We all know it steals the true spirit of Christmas. Yet, year after year it happens.

Advent—the season of waiting and preparing for the coming of the Messiah, the Christ child, Immanuel, God with us here and now. The wonder of God's coming to us in the form of that tiny, very human baby, the essence of the gospel, captures us all. Our traditions add to the meaning of the season and enrich our experience of it. They draw us together as friends and as family. Persons reach out to one another with a warmth not seen or felt at other times of the year. So where does the Christmas Crunch fit in? Is this what we associate with Advent, those holy weeks leading up to Christmas? Could it be that in those weeks the crunch overshadows the crèche?

Here is an active Advent experience designed to assist youth or adults in sorting through their values at this season. It focuses on the contrast between the Christmas of the shopping mall and that of the sanctuary. It might be done on a Friday evening, a Saturday afternoon and evening, or even a Sunday. It will take a good chunk of time to allow for an outing as well as some activities back at the church, but the process is an essential part of the learning and promises to enrich the Advent experience of all who participate.

The Event—Part 1

Gather at the church and prepare to go to a nearby shopping mall or a downtown shopping area. If you live in a rural area, this may mean some travel, but that adds to the adventure, too. If your group is large, divide into smaller groups or have each person choose a partner for the outing. Then make the following assignments for each group or pair to accomplish.

1. Spend a half hour just walking and observing people, interactions, shopping styles, signs, and so forth.

2. Spend the next half hour taking notes about what you've seen and heard. In particular, deal with these questions:
    * What are the key slogans? What are they saying about gift giving?
    * What kinds of gifts are merchants "pushing" this year?
    * What are the signs of Christmas here? What creates the magic?
    * What kinds of interactions do you see between persons?

3. Spend the next half hour conducting "person-in-the-mall"/"person-on-the-street" interviews. Make up some of your own questions or use the following:

- What do you enjoy most about this season?
- What concerns you most about this season?
- Do you enjoy shopping for friends, family? What kinds of gifts do you plan to give this year?
- How do you see the meaning of Christmas?

Encourage consideration and prudence in approaching interviewees. Suggest that persons introduce themselves and talk with people of all ages, even a clerk if they can find one free.

Gauge the time of each of the three assignments according to your schedule.

The Event—Part 2

Return to the church and have the participants go directly to the sanctuary (or wherever your church's center of Christmas celebration may be). Ask them to spend the next five to ten minutes sitting quietly, reflecting on the experience thus far, taking in the new surroundings. Then break the silence by reading the Christmas story as told in Luke 2:1–14.

Do some talking together about the Christmas traditions in your church. What are some of the signs of Christmas here? Ask them to relate some of their favorite Christmas memories and traditions associated with the church.

Now, do some debriefing about the mall or downtown experience. Ask for reports from their note taking and interviewing. What did they see, hear, feel, wonder?

It should be noted that shopping areas are not all bad. However, for Christians and non-Christians alike, they seem to capture the essence of the commercialism that has come to be associated with the Christmas season and often detracts from the true spirit of this holy season, the season of preparing for Christmas and Christ's coming.

Sing a Christmas carol or two and then prepare to move on to the third and final part of the event.

The Event—Part 3

This part of the event is designed to help the participants put together the observations and learnings of the total event in a very real and tangible way as well as to provide some additional fun and festivity.

Four activity centers are suggested. These will need to have been prepared in advance in an area where you can spread out. Check the Bible references at the end of this article for use in centers #1 and #2. Depending on the size of the group, you may choose to do all four activity centers, dividing the total group into four small groups. Or with a smaller group you may want to choose to do one or two of the activities as a total group.

Activity Center #1

Create posters that capture the spirit of Advent. These may warn persons of the danger of the Christmas Crunch or give suggestions about styles of gift giving. Put these posters up around the church for the duration of Advent.

Activity Center #2

Create a commercial, skit, or pantomime that expresses the learning of this event. For example, participants may contrast the Christmas of the shopping mall with that of the church or focus on preserving the best and truest spirit of Christmas. Perhaps these "brief commercial announcements" could be done for an adult or younger Sunday school class, in morning worship, or at some other all-church gathering.

Activity Center #3

Make symbolic gifts such as peace, hope, strength, or encouragement. How? Only your imagination limits you! Make plans to give these very real gifts away, perhaps to persons of special need within the congregation.

Activity Center #4

Make some actual gifts to be given to friends or family members. Perhaps people skilled in crafts could teach others to make candles, minibanners, wreaths, or other crafts. The best gifts are those that come from the hearts and hands of people dear to you.

How does one conclude such an event as this? With celebration, that's how! Share the products of the activity centers. Put up the posters; try out the commercials. Sing some more Christmas carols together or play some Christmas music. And for a finale, some sugar-coated, calorie-laden Christmas goodies seem to be in order!

Bible References on Giving

Isaiah 9:6	The Messiah is given, a gift.
Genesis 28:22	We give out of what God has given us.
Matthew 10:8	Freely have you received; so you should freely give.
John 14:27	Jesus gives as the world does not/cannot give.
Acts 20:32–35	Happiness is in giving.
Matthew 6:2–4	Give in secret; don't be "showy."
Ephesians 2:8–10	Salvation is a gift.
Mark 14:3–9	Jesus receives a gift.
Matthew 2:1–12	The Magi brought gifts.

CHRISTMAS GOODIES
To Make and Give

A Project for the Whole Family

from Margaret Anne Huffman

Good Neighbor Nine-Bean Soup Mix

Mix equal portions of dried beans (lima, navy, pinto, black, kidney, and white northern), green split peas, black-eyed peas, and lentils.

Let children measure two cups of bean mix into quart-sized plastic bags. Or layer the beans in glass pint jars, allowing $\frac{1}{4}$ cup per variety. Make a copy of the recipe right and attach it to each jar or bag with a holiday ribbon. When delivering, include a loaf of homemade bread or a batch of Christmas Croutons (recipe below).

Nine-Bean Soup

- 2 cups bean mix
- 2 quarts water
- 1 pound ham, diced
- 16-ounce can tomatoes, undrained and chopped
- 10-ounce can green chiles, undrained
- $\frac{1}{2}$–$\frac{1}{3}$ teaspoon salt
- 1 clove garlic, minced
- 1 onion, chopped

Sort and wash beans and place in Dutch oven. Cover with water two inches over beans and soak overnight. Drain; add the 2 quarts of water, ham, onion, garlic and salt. Cover; bring to boil and reduce heat, simmering 1½ hours or until beans are tender. Add remaining ingredients. Makes about 8 cups.

Christmas Croutons

- A loaf of good-quality, dense white bread
- Miniature Christmas cookie cutters (1-inch size)—star, bell, angel, gingerbread man, or whatever you can find
- $\frac{1}{2}$ cup butter
- $\frac{1}{4}$ cup olive oil
- 2–3 minced garlic cloves

Cut out shapes from bread. In a large skillet melt the butter with the oil; add the garlic. Carefully toss in the bread cutouts, being careful not to crowd them. Brown on both sides; use tongs to gently turn each crouton. Cool them on paper towel. Store in an airtight container. Serve with salad or with Nine-Bean Soup.

Other Recipes

Cherry Christmas Cake
from Beverly Carlson

Beat together:
- 4 eggs
- 1/3 cup orange juice
- 1½ cups sugar
- 1 tablespoon vanilla

Mix and set aside:
- ½ cup sugar
- 1 teaspoon cinnamon
- 1 can cherry pie filling

Mix the following dry ingredients until well blended and add oil gradually.
- 2 teaspoons baking powder
- 1 teaspoon salt
- 3 cups flour
- 1 cup vegetable oil

Blend egg mixture into oil and dry ingredients.

Preheat oven to 350°. Grease and flour a tube pan with a removable bottom. Put half the batter in. Arrange half the pie filling on top. Sprinkle half the cinnamon sugar mixture on top of the cherries. Repeat with the rest of the batter, sugar mixture, and cherries. Bake for one hour or until done.

This is a delicious and attractive cake that requires no frosting. Cherry and strawberry fillings are colorful at Christmas. You can also use apple, blueberry, peach, or apricot; dark sweet cherry is especially good.

Braided Christmas Bread

This bread can be as easy or as complicated as you want to make it. The recipe given here is simple enough for children.

- 1 loaf frozen bread dough, thawed (or mix your own dough)
- Any of the following goodies:

  > brown sugar
  > cinnamon
  > pinches of cardamom, ginger, nutmeg, clove
  > raisins or currants
  > cranberries
  > chopped nuts
  > fruit pie filling *(apple and cherry are good)*

Divide the dough in half; it will make two loaves. Roll out dough into a vertical rectangle. Spread your goodies along the center third of the rectangle. With a table knife, cut horizontal strips at one-inch intervals on the two outer thirds. Then, beginning at the top, fold each strip over the center, alternating right and left. Angle the strips down a little, and you will get a braided effect. Brush the top with beaten egg. Bake according to the frozen dough directions.

Just for Kids

Kids' Cheese Nut Fudge

from Margaret Anne Huffman

- 3-ounce package cream cheese
- 2 cups powdered sugar
- 1 square melted unsweetened chocolate
- chopped nuts

Mix well, squeezing with your hands. Pat onto a plate and cut into squares or roll in small balls. Refrigerate.

Peanut Butter Creams

from Margaret Anne Huffman

- $\frac{1}{4}$ cup powdered sugar
- 1 cup chocolate chips
- $\frac{1}{2}$ cup sweetened condensed milk
- 1 cup creamy peanut butter

Mix well with hands and shape into balls. Store in airtight container.

SONGS OF THE
SEASON

Children's Song of the Nativity

1. How far is it to Beth-le-hem? Not ve-ry far. Shall
3. May we stroke the crea-tures there. Ox, ass, or sheep? May
5. —— Great kings have pre-cious gifts, And we have naught, ____

we find the sta-ble-room Lit by a star? 2. Can we see the
we peep like them and see Je-sus a-sleep? 4. If we touch his
Little smiles and little tears Are all__ we brought. 6. For all wea-ry
7. ____God in his

lit-tle child, Is he with-in? If we lift the wood-en latch May we go in?
ti-ny hand Will he a-wake? Will he know we've come so far Just for his sake?
chil-dren Ma-ry must weep. __ Here, on his bed of straw Sleep, chil-dren, sleep.
mother's arms Babes in the byre, __ Sleep, as they sleep who find Their heart's de-sire.

Words: Frances Chesterton

Music: English Traditional

Long Ago There Was Born

Words: P.W. Blackmer

Music: Johannes Brahms

From *Who Is God* Perspectives 1, Semester 1, Faith and Work Graded Series ©1969, used by permission of the American Baptist Board of Education and Publication

Sing of the Baby

Oh we sing____ of the ba - by, ba - by Je - sus

born to - day In a man - ger, in a man - ger,

far a - way____ far a - way. O'er the man - ger,

O'er the man - ger in the sky a shi - ny star

Guides the wise men to the ba - by in a man - ger

filled with hay. Sing! Sing! of the ba - by

in the man - ger far a - way Sing! Sing!

of the ba - by. Born for us on Christ - mas day!

From *Wondering About God* Perspectives 1, Semester 1, Faith and Work Graded Series ©1969, used by permission of the American Baptist Board of Education and Publication

Contributors

JULIA BEBEAU Having previously served as a communications specialist, associate pastor, and chaplain, Julia Bebeau works as a pastoral counselor. Each Christmas, she continues to negotiate the dance between shopping mall and sanctuary—the FBC of Cumberland in Indianapolis.

BEVERLY CLARK CARLSON recently retired as executive director of The American Baptist Historical Society. Her husband, Allen, is a retired college administrator. They have a son and two daughters pursuing careers in medicine, international development, and ministry.

SUSAN KATHLEEN CASEY has a B.A. in History and Theatre from the College of William and Mary and an M.Div. from Fuller Theological Seminary. She edits marketing materials for a pharmaceutical company and is an active member of the First Presbyterian Church of Phoenixville, Pennsylvania. She writes, "Most of my Christmas ornaments are gifts or travel souvenirs, so decorating the tree means remembering special people and times—and giving thanks."

ARTHUR F. FOGARTIE is a fourth-generation Presbyterian minister. He received his B.A. from the University of North Carolina and his M.Div. from Princeton Theological Seminary. He currently serves the First Presbyterian Church of Lynchburg, Virginia, and it is his custom to write a Christmas story as his annual gift to his congregation.

RANDY FRAME is acquisitions editor at Judson Press and is the spouse of this volume's editor. Once as a child he ran downstairs to check his stocking on Christmas morn and found a big diamond in the making (a lump of coal), which years later he admits he deserved.

ISRAEL GALINDO is a Christian educator living in Virginia. He and his wife, Barbara, have two boys, Douglas and Thomas. His book *The Craft of Christian Teaching* has recently been published by Judson Press. The Galindos enjoy extending the Christmas holiday by observing Advent through Epiphany, including the festive twelfth night feast at their church.

LUCIA HERNDON is a family columnist for *The Philadelphia Inquirer*. She and her husband, Hal Horning, are native Iowans who live in Philadelphia with their two children, Melissa, 21, and Timothy, 16. Herndon believes that "keeping Christmas in the heart year-round is a year-round occupation. "The Christmas List" is reprinted by permission from *The Philadelphia Inquirer*.

LEE HILL-NELSON is a mother of three and grandmother of four. She is a retired church secretary and a member of the First United Methodist Church in Waco, Texas. She and her husband spend their vacations in Crested Butte, Colorado. About Christmas she writes, "I love the season because we draw near to Christ, and because it is a time when we hear from out-of-town friends. As a tradition, we have made candy

cane cookies for the past 40 years and continue to do so. We also attend the candlelight service on Christmas Eve."

GARTH HOUSE is a freelance writer who lives in Columbus, Ohio, with his two cats, Missy and Hiawatha. Having battled major mental illness for 20 years, Garth finds the Christmas season a time to wonder at the birth of healing into the world and into his own life.

MARGARET ANNE HUFFMAN, Shelbyville, Indiana, award-winning journalist, is author of *Through the Valley: Prayers for Violent Times* and *When Illness Comes* (Judson), as well as 17 other books. She's currently working on a cozy mystery series. She and husband, Rev. Gary Huffman (PCUSA), have three children—Beth, Rob, and Lynn James— and two grandchildren, Aaron and Kali. She braces herself each December, for "Christmas brings the unexpected...frozen water pipes during the church caroling supper in our part-log home on the Big Blue River, a kitty lost (found!) in the snow, and owls caroling from snowy treetops."

J. LYNN JAMES The Rev. Lynn James, LCPC, is an ordained American Baptist minister working part-time as a co-pastor with her husband, Rev. Dr. Jack Skiles, in Mt. Prospect, Illinois. She works full-time as a licensed clinical professional counselor in private practice, specializing in working with survivors of interpersonal violence. She is the mother of Kali, age 7, and stepmother of Aaron, age 16. She writes, "Every Christmas the family gathers to stick all kinds of candy on the gingerbread houses lovingly created by my parents Margaret Anne (who is also a contributor to this book) and Gary Huffman (and then we eat the rooftops!)."

JEFFREY D. JONES is currently director of Educational Ministries' Department of Education for Discipleship and the ServiceCenter, American Baptist Churches, U.S.A. He previously served as pastor of the First Baptist Church in Chili, New York and the First Baptist Church of Pitman, New Jersey.

WILLIAM D. KENNEDY Bill Kennedy is a storyteller and church songwriter who practices law for a living. Every year, to celebrate Christmas with his friends and church family, he writes a new account about the people of fictional Yellow Springs "where ordinary people do the extraordinary and sometimes learn something along the way." Bill lives in Malvern, Pennsylvania, with his wife and daughters.

GARY L. McCANN is senior minister of New England Congregational Church in Aurora, Illinois. "Hanging of the Greens" originally appeared in the Fall 1990 issue of *Baptist Leader*.

ELLA PEARSON MITCHELL & HENRY H. MITCHELL Ella Muriel Pearson and Henry H. Mitchell met at Union Theological Seminary in New York City in 1941, and were married there in 1944. They have lived and served in Durham, North Carolina; Berkeley, Fresno, and Santa Monica, California; Rochester, New York; Richmond, Virginia; and Atlanta, Georgia. They earned their doctorates at Claremont School of Theology. They have three living children and six grandchildren. "Jesus' Birthday at Our House" first appeared in the Christmas-focused October–December 1995 issue of *The Living Pulpit*.

LUTHER C. PIERCE The Rev. Luther C. Pierce is a retired United Church of Christ pastor who lives with his wife, Frances, in the small Berkshire town of Cummington, Massachusetts. Their four grown sons are scattered up and down the East Coast. Rev. Pierce stays busy by preaching, writing, woodworking, and caring for his garden and flock of bantams and pheasants. His Christmas sermons, stories, and poems seek to call people away from secular celebrations and toward the Light that shines in the Incarnation. The liturgies for Advent are taken from his Advent devotional booklet, *Christmas Giving,* previously published by Rev. Luther C. Pierce.

ROBERT S. REID Bob was pastor of Sixth Avenue Baptist Church in Tacoma when he wrote "Does Santa Belong in Church." Now he teaches communication at St. Martin's College in Washington state and is adjunct in speech and homiletics for Fuller Theological Seminary. His children, Laura and Matt, are teenagers now, but friends still ask, "Hey! What's up with getting presents on December 6th?" That's when friends get to hear the story of the "real" Santa.

KENNETH L. SEHESTED is executive director and editor of the Baptist Peace Fellowship of North America and recipient of the 1995 Dahlberg Peace Award from the American Baptist Churches, U.S.A. He is married to Nancy Hastings Sehested, pastor of Sweet Fellowship Baptist Church in Clyde, North Carolina, and has two daughters. His special Christmas ritual is to design a Sehested family Christmas card, including an original poem. "Boundary to Benedictus: A Meditation on Zechariah" came from his 1997 Christmas card.

JODY SEYMOUR is senior minister of First United Methodist Church in Gastonia, North Carolina. A certified Enneagram personality and spirituality instructor, he conducts renewal retreats for laity and clergy and is author of *Looking for God in All the Wrong Places* and *A Time for Healing: Overcoming the Perils of Ministry* (both published by Judson Press).